True Love Has a Passion for You!

Second Edition

By

His Utility Handmaiden,

Gail P. Miller

Published by

Queen V Publishing
Dayton, Ohio
QueenVPublishing.com

Published by

Queen V Publishing
Dayton, Ohio
QueenVPublishing.com
Info@PenOfTheWriter.com

Copyright © 2005 by Gail P. Miller

All rights reserved. No part of this book may be reproduced or transmitted in any form or by any means, electronic or mechanical, without prior written consent of the Publisher, except for the inclusion of brief quotes in a review.

Scripture taken from the New Kings James Version®. Copyright © 1982 by Thomas Nelson, Inc. Used by permission. All rights reserved.

James Strong LL.D., S.T.D. *The New Strong's Exhaustive Concordance of the Bible*, Nashville, Tennessee, by Thomas Nelson Publishers, 1990.

Thompson Nelson Bibles. *New Spirit Filled Life Bible*, Nashville, TN 1982, 2002

New King James Version, *Spirit Filled Life Bible for Students*, Nashville, Atlanta, London, Vancouver, by Thomas Nelson Publishers, 1995.

Library of Congress Control Number: 2008943538
ISBN-13: 978-0-9794489-1-1

Cover designer: Keith Saunders of Marion Designs
Editor: Valerie J. Lewis Coleman of Pen of the Writer
Author photographer: Melvin Williams of His Majesty's Image

Printed in the United States of America

Acknowledgements

My gratitude to my pastor, sister, long time friend and spiritual mother Dr. Diane M. Parks-Love, who first read and typed this work for me. Thank you for walking with me, feeding me, correcting me, challenging me, counseling me, and making sure I gave **God** nothing less then excellence. Thank you for being patient with me, not giving up on me and teaching me the uncompromised truth which is causing me continued growth and maturity in the ways and service of **God**.

Thank you, Jerilyn Hampton-Sawyer, for writing the introduction, editing and refining this work. Much thanks to Denise Alexander and Connie Beal for coming on board to bring **God's** message to fruition.

Thanks to Mrs. George W. Lucas, Pastor Charles & Joan Brown, Pastor Titus & Jackie Patrick, Pastor George & Katherine Hawkins, Pastors Ivan & Gloria Love, Pastor Timothy & Tonya Biggers, Pastor Larry & Stephanie Nelms, Pastor Eddie & Jacqueline Jaudon, Roger & Sharon Neal, Karen Mckenzie, Jacqueline Colbert, Shavon Norvell, Evelyn Buchanan, Hermita Dees-Brown, Megan Edmonds, Jocelyn Love, Destiny Love, Bernadeita Laury Bro. Andre Sims, and my brother Glen, who designed the initial cover for this book.

Thank you Rev. Thelma Buchanan and Kimberly Miller for your prayers, care, help and trusted friendship at this point in my life.

Thanks to Brother Steve Arrington, for blazing a trail to the presents of **God** that sparked my hunger for **His** presence, intimacy and the deep things of **God's** heart.

To Karen Battle, Sheila McCray, Janice Colvin, Donald & Frances Winborn, Peter & Shawn Pullen, Vernon Richardson, Sheryl Davis, Mildred Johnson, Sheila Nixon, Doris Johnson, Vernell Tate, Valeria Wilson, Sheila Baggett, Sherry Holliday, and Ms. Moore thanks for just being there.

Dedication

I dedicate this book in memory of my loving parents, George & Albertha Miller, who lived a life of commitment to **God** and each other for 51 years. To my late aunts and uncles, William & Geneva McNeil, Leroy Thompson, Cleveland Miller, Bertram Miller, Levi Miller, Al Miyara, and my late grandmothers Eliza T. Hall and Bertha D. Miller.

I also dedicate this message to the memories of Lisa R. Rucker, Michael D. Wright, Dr. Robert B. Robinson and Elder Charles Anderson, Jr. You are all missed greatly.

To my dear son, Darrell N. Miller, who has been a joy and gift to me from the Lord. You have given me the blessing of being a grandmother to Darrell N. Miller II and Jarrell N. Miller. Also, to Alishia Wood-Miller who is like a daughter to me, thank you for hanging in there.

To my brothers and their families, George & Marcia N. Miller Jr., Brianan, Grace, George III, Glen & Tierney A. Miller, Marcus & April Carr, Glen Q., Angelo, Dameka, Shaun, Kylie, Cerenity, and all my other family members throughout the United States and the Bahamas.

To the staff and students at Cornell Heights, Wogaman Elementary and Dayton Dunbar High School whose lives have been instrumental in developing me as a teacher, coach, friend and person.

To Rev. Cindy Taylor, all my sisters and brothers in the Lord, classmates at Liberated in Christ School of Ministry and to people everywhere this book is dedicated to **you.**

His Utility Handmaiden

God named me *His Utility Handmaiden* from a place of brokenness. Like a wall outlet that has nothing to do with the power that comes through it or what is being plugged in it, I am there to release the power. Like the spout on a sink that cannot turn on or off by itself and has nothing to do with how much water flows through it, I am there to give water; for cleansing or to quench thirst. I am like the receiver on a phone waiting for someone to pick it up. I have nothing to do with what is being said, I serve only as a conduit to deliver the message.

God later revealed that people have utility closets in their homes filled with a variety of tools. **He** also called me **His** *Cornucopia*. So, in essence, I am a tool in **God's** hand ready to be used for **His** purpose and endowed with the fruit of **His** Spirit.

The major knowledge that the **Reader** must understand about this invitation is that **God, Himself,** is speaking. Even the *Songs of Gail* are the direct result of the **Holy Spirit**'s planting in my heart and are the first fruits of our holy union.

True Love Has a Passion for You!

Gail P. Miller

Table of Contents

Foreword vii
Introduction ix
True Love Has a Passion for You! 1
True Love Fills the Gap 5
True Love Desires to Possess You! 7
Why Do You Reject Me? 13
True Love Creates 17
Just Think! 21
What You Need is Me! 25
I Can't Choose for You! 31
I Already Love You! 35
Prophetic Poetic Mysteries 43
   Word of the Lord! 1 46
      Dr. Diane Parks-Love 46
   Whose House is It Anyway? 48
   I Don't Know You! 51
   Alliances! 54
   I Don't Need! 56
   Consider This! 58
   My Holiness 60
   Intimacy with God! 61
   Word of the Lord! 2 62
   Word of the Lord! 3 63
   Do You Love Me My Way? 67
   When It's Time, I Will Bring It to Pass! 69
   Cry Out to Me! 72
   Seek Me to Find Out Who You Are! 74
   I Own It All 76
   My Heart Aches! 77
   Give Me a Chance! 78
   Bring Me Your Heart! 79
   Come Rest 80
   Freely! 81
   No Matter What! 82
   I Just Wanted to Say 83
   Dwelling Place 84
   Those Same People! 85

True Love Has a Passion for You!

Songs of the Lord & Songs of Gail 87
   Broken by the Lord 88
   Sing Songs 89
   Great Joy! 90
   Let Him Have His Way! 91
   The Lord by His Spirit is Moving! 92
   The Daughters of the Lord! 94
   She Speaks 95
   Love is Stronger! 96
   Healing is the Children's Bread 98
   Only You! 99
   Open Your Heart! 100
   How Great is Our God? 102
   Sing to the Lord! 103
   Stand in the Name of Jesus 105
   God and You! 106
   True Love Opened My Heart! 107
   The God of Power! 108
   Here Am I Lord! 109
   What Can I Do? 110
   Blow On Your Garden! 111
   My Heart 112
   He Took Me! 113
Words of Wisdom, Knowledge and Exhortation 115
   Denominationalism 116
   But God Said! 121
   Forgive 123
   His Song! 124
   His Voice! 125
   He's Calling You! 126
   He's Calling for Holy People! 127
   Is Your Name Written? 130
   What Excuse Will You Give? 132
   If God Be for You! 133
   You Are Nothing Without Him! 135
   You Are! 136
   You Are His Bride! 137
   He Has a Right! 141
   Are You Sleeping with Your Sister? 142
   Your Sin! 143
   Separated from Him 145
   You Can Give! 147

Are You Keeping Him from What He Deserves? 149
Give Him What He Asks For! 150
The King's Table! 151
The Presence of God 152
Fellowship 153
His Blood 154
The Blood Speaks! 155
Grace 156
God the Butcher 157
The Carcass 159
In Him! 160
Who Is Jesus? 161
He Is 166
He was Slain 167
Silently! 168
He's Coming Soon! 169
The Choice 170
The Seed! 171
The Blessing! 173
Change 174
It's About Him! 175
Press In! 176
Springs of the Heart! 178
Waiting for You! 179
You Have a Right to His Love! 180
You Have Him Forever! 182
He Chose You! 184
True Love Knew You When! 185
He Made You! 186
Imagine That!!! 188
Boundaries 189
How Is! 190
Before! 191
True Love Brings! 192
A Different Realm 193
Things 194
Living Water! 195
Fragrance of Christ 197
That Day! 198
What Do You Want? 200
Divine Revelation 201
My Father 203

Bibliography 207
About Gail P. Miller 209
Queen V Publishing 211

Gail P. Miller

Foreword

By Dr. Diane Parks-Love, M.M., D.D

There are goods books and there are great books, *True Love Has a Passion for You!,* is an awesome book written with a taste of the supernatural. This book has a natural author, Gail P. Miller, however the primary author is the LORD GOD and thus, the supernatural surfaces in this work.

True Love transports the reader into the heart of God. You will experience the genuine love of a Creator for His creation. You will be touched by the desire of God to demonstrate His Passion for man. You will see your life and natural attempts to find true love, then you will understand that what you sought—True Love—can only be experienced inside the Love of God.

There is sensual love; there is brotherly love; but Agapé is the love that asks only to be accepted. Agapé is the love that **God** gives in spite of who we are or are not. Agapé love offers to transform us into the vessels that we were born to be, according to God's purpose. Agapé love defines Truth. Truth being: *"For God so loved the world that He gave..."* Agapé love gave Christ, Jesus to the world. Agapé love is supernatural and indefinable. Agapé is true Passion.

Enter and be caressed by the heart of God. Enter and receive that which was purposed for you from the foundation of the world. Enter and be blessed!

Yours in Christ,

Dr. Diane M. Parks-Love, pastor
Liberated In Christ Ministries, Inc. Dayton, Ohio

True Love Has a Passion for You!

Gail P. Miller

Introduction

The Creator placed within each of us a yearning; which some may define as a quest or thirst to pursue what seems unobtainable. During our journey we find ourselves crossing the path of others, who are apprehending what we desire. They display a fulfillment we have been trying to obtain. They know our Creator alone can satisfy this yearning!

Without the guidance of my spirit, I pursued people, places and things to quench my thirst. When I followed its guidance, I found myself being lead to others who are living fulfilled lives, by submitting their will to the Master. The handmaiden of this inspiration of God is one of those people. She is my teacher, and a precious gift God, has molded just for this purpose.

Sister Miller is reserved in her appearance, and exudes strength and humility in her presence. She has the ability to listen, give and repent when she has been disobedient. To summarize her, she is on a peaceful journey, satisfied with her path and focused on her pursuit. She is obedient to the will of her Maker. Pursuing her call, Sister Miller is pressing toward the mark of the high calling in Christ Jesus.

After reading this book changes will occur in your life! I pray that one day your journey will lead you to someone who is obediently doing God's will. You will recognize them because they glow from an inner beauty. The Holy Spirit working from within is the source of this illumination.

Lovingly submitted,

Jerilyn Hampton-Sawyer

True Love Has a Passion for You!

Gail P. Miller

Chapter One
True Love Has a Passion for You!

First, **you** need to know **True Love** is a **Who** and not just emotions. **True Love** has feelings and expressions, which is a part of what comes out of **True Love**, but **True Love**, is a **Who**.[1] Since we know **True Love** is a **Who**, we can safely say **True Love** has a voice. Because **True Love** has a voice, there is something **True Love** would like to say to **you**.[2]

Now, **I** would like for **you** to meet **True Love**. **True Love**, this is the **reader**. **Reader**, this **is True Love!**

"Pleased to meet **you, reader**." I have waited for a long time to meet with **you** and have a chance to talk to **you**. I know what **you** have seen; I know what **you** heard and I know what **you** believe about **Me**. But **I, Myself**, have a desire to reveal **Who** I really am to **you**.

I don't want **you** to go by what **you** have seen, heard or even learned from others. I want **you** to know from **Me Who** I really am. I want **you** to know how much I desire to give **Myself** to **you**.

> **I want you to know**
> I have *always* wanted *you.*
> **I want you to know**
> I have *always* wanted to be *your friend.*
> **I want you to know**
> I have *always* wanted to be *your* **first** *love.*

My love for you has no boundaries. If *you* allow **Me**, **I** can be everything and anything **you** need **Me** to be! That's why **I** have come today to speak to **you** as if we were, **face** to **face**.[3]

1

True Love Has a Passion for You!

I desire you. You didn't know it, but **I** have been **Here** all the time. **You** don't know *Me*, but **I** sure know *you*! **I** have been following **you**, in fact, **I** have been looking for **you** and at **you** everyday! [4] However, **I** desire to let **you** know that *I have a passion for you*!

This word **"Passion"** means real powerful feeling, liking and suffering.[a]

I have strong feelings for **you**. **My** emotions are so strong they have caused **Me** to draw **you** near **My** presence today. **I** also like **you** and **I** like being with **you**. **I** like looking at **you** and **I** desire a close relationship with **you**.

There is a part of **Me** that was willing to suffer for **you**. **I AM** still willing to take pain, harm, loss and injury just for **you**. The reason why **I AM** so willing to take all of this for **you** is because of **My** strong desire for **your** friendship. [5]

You see, **I** wanted **you** before **you** even knew **Who I** was! All **I** ask is that **you** give **Me** a chance to reveal to **you, Who I** really am. If **you** find **I AM** not **Who I** say **I AM, you** have the right to choose something or someone else, and *I* will respect **your** choice!

I have a strong desire to have a sincere kinship with **you**. **I** just want someone **I** can trust with the deep things within **My** Heart. The things **I** won't tell just anyone. **I** want someone to be honest with **Me**. **I** want someone who won't try to cover things up. These things **you** try to keep secret will only cause **you** hurt and in turn, hurt **Me**. This is because dishonesty separates **you** from **Me**, and **I** don't want **us** to be separated any more.

I, True Love, want someone to believe in **Me**. Someone to believe **I** can do what **I** say **I** can do, and to believe **I** really want to.

Everybody desires *someone* to believe in them.

I want **you** to know **I** will do **you** right, because **I** declare things that are right.

    I won't
        *lie on **you**.*

    I won't
        *cheat on **you**.*

Gail P. Miller

I won't
        take advantage of you.

I will *never*
        leave you.

I will *never*
        forsake you.

I will *never*
        stop loving you.[6]

    There is no failure in True Love. Anything **you** try to hide from **Me**, **I** already know! **You** don't have to be afraid of **Me** because **True Love** gets rid of all fears. Any fears **you** have, **I** will take care of them. Therefore, getting rid of all **you**r fears allows **you** to trust **Me** so that our relationship can be unlimited.

    You must understand there is nothing **I** have not given up for **you**. All **I** have, **I** have already given **for us to be together**. If **you** choose **Me,** there will be no end to **our** relationship! There is nothing that will ever be able to separate **My Love** from **you**.

True Love Has a Passion for You!

Nothing **you** have said or done in the past
will ever separate **My Love** from **you**.
Nothing **you** will say or do tomorrow
will ever separate **My Love** from **you**.
Not even death or life shall be able to
separate **My Love** from **you**
or keep **Me** from truly **loving you!**[7]

Gail P. Miller

True Love Fills the Gap

Washinggggggggggggggggggggg

Healinggggggggggggggggggggg

Onenessssssssssssssssssssssssss

Loveeeeeeeeeeeeeeeeeeeeeeeee

Empowermentttttttttttttttttttttttttt

Nourishmentttttttttttttttttttttttttt

Encouragementttttttttttttttttttttttt

Strengthhhhhhhhhhhhhhhhhhhh

Salvationnnnnnnnnnnnnnnnnnn

"**Gap**" means an empty, separated, broken, unfulfilled place or space.[b]
True Love <u>alone</u> can and will fill it for **you,** but only if *you* permit. **I AM** committed to **you** as well as loving **you.** True Love is everywhere at all times.
Right where you are now,
True Love
is.

True Love Has a Passion for You!

Scripture Reference

Footnote 1	Genesis 1:26-27
	I John 4:7-8
	I John 4:16
Footnote 2	Genesis 1:28-29
	Luke 4:18-19
	John 1:1-3
Footnote 3	Exodus 33:11
	Jeremiah 31:3
	Romans 5:8
Footnote 4	Genesis 1:26-27
	Ephesians 2:10
	Revelation 1:8
Footnote 5	Isaiah 53:4-5
	Proverbs 18:24
	John 15:13
Footnote 6	Genesis 3:8
	Isaiah 45:19
	Hebrews 13:5
Footnote 7	Exodus 3:14
	Romans 8:35-39
	I John 4:18-19

Chapter Two
True Love Desires to Possess You!

The word "**Possess**" means to preserve, own, keep up, support or occupy.^c

True Love paid the ultimate price for **you**. I gave, *My only Love* to be one with **you**, just so **you** can be like **Me**! **You** are able to pursue **Me** at **your** will. **I AM** here for **you**, merely for the asking, with a strong desire to **possess you**.[8]

> **I, True Love,** desire...
> > to **possess your** will.
>
> **I, True Love,** desire...
> > to **possess your** mind.
>
> **I, True Love,** desire...
> > to **possess your** soul.
>
> **I, True Love,** desire...
> > to **possess your** heart.
>
> **I, True Love,** desire...
> > to **possess your** body.
>
> **I, True Love,** desire...
> > to **possess your** strength.
>
> **I, True Love,** desire...
> > to **possess your** emotions.
>
> **I, True Love,** desire...
> > to **possess your** passions.
>
> **I, True Love,** desire...
> > to **possess your** hunger.
>
> **I, True Love,** desire...

to **possess your** thirst.
I, True Love, desire…
to **possess your** appetite.
I, True Love, desire…
to **possess your** habits.
I, True Love, desire…
to **possess your** thoughts.
I, True Love, desire…
to **possess your** ways.
I, True Love, desire…
to **possess your** behavior.
I, True Love, desire…
to **possess your** personality.
I, True Love, desire…
to **possess your** character.
I, True Love, desire…
to **possess your** ego.
I, True Love, desire…
to **possess your** perception.
I, True Love, desire…
to **possess your** imagination.
I, True Love, desire…
to **possess your** possessions.
I, True Love, desire…
to **possess your** past.
I, True Love, desire…
to **possess your** present.
I, True Love, desire…
to **possess your** future.
I, True Love, desire…
to **possess your** life.

I, True Love, desire…

to possess all of You!

Gail P. Miller

If **I occupy** all of **you**, then **I Am** able to get what **I need**. Yes, I have **needs** and **My need** is to **occupy you**. **You** see…

If **I occupy your will**, I can get out of **your will** what
I *planned.*
If **I occupy your mind**, I can get out of **your mind** what
    I *planned.*
If **I occupy your soul**, I can get out of **your soul** what
        I *planned.*
If **I occupy your heart**, I can get out of **your heart** what
            I *planned.*
If **I occupy your body**, I can get out of **your body** what
                I *planned.*
If **I occupy your strength**, I can get out of **your strength** what
                    I *planned.*
If **I occupy your emotions**, I can get out of **your emotions** what
                        I *planned.*
If **I occupy your passions**, I can get out of **your passions** what
                            I *planned.*
If **I occupy your hunger**, I can get out of **your hunger** what
                                I *planned.*
If **I occupy your thirst**, I can get out of **your thirst** what
                                    I *planned.*
If **I occupy your appetite**, I can get out of **your appetite** what
                                      I *planned.*
If **I occupy your habits**, I can get out of **your habits** what
                                          I *planned.*
If **I occupy your thoughts**, I can get out of **your thoughts** what
I *planned.*

True Love Has a Passion for You!

If **I occupy your ways**, **I** can get out of **your ways** what
  I *planned.*
If **I occupy your personality**, **I** can get out of **your personality** what
  I *planned.*
If **I occupy your character**, **I** can get out of **your character** what
  I *planned.*
If **I occupy your ego**, **I** can get out of **your ego** what
  I *planned.*
If **I occupy your perception**, **I** can get out of **your perception** what
  I *planned.*
If **I occupy your imagination**, **I** can get out of **your imagination** what
  I *planned.*
If **I occupy your possessions**, **I** can get out of **your possessions** what
  I *planned.*
If **I occupy your past**, then **I** can get out of **your past** what
  I *planned.*
If **I occupy your present**, **I** can get out of **your present** what
  I *planned.*
If **I occupy your future**, **I** can get out of **your future** what
  I *planned.*
If **I occupy your life**, **I** can get out of **your life** what
  I *planned.*
If **I occupy you**, then...

I've got *My* Plan!*[9]*

Gail P. Miller

I form images of **Myself** on whatever **I** come in contact with. Just one touch, leaves **My** imprint upon **you**. However, **I** cannot **possess** any part of **your** heart, soul, mind, or body without **your** consent. **I do not force Myself on anyone!** True Love gives!

There is no getting over **True Love!**
There is no getting under **True Love!**
There is no getting around **True Love!**
There is no falling through **True Love!**

There is no end to True Love!

Nothing is lost in **True Love** because **True Love owns all.**

The results of **True Love** take **you** beyond this natural world.

You begin to **talk** like **True Love**.

    You begin to **walk** like **True Love**.

        You begin to **look** like **True Love**.

            You begin to **act** like **True Love**.

                You begin to **obey** the voice of **True Love**.

True Love is the fulfillment of love Bodily.[10]

True Love Has a Passion for You!

Scripture Reference

Footnote 8 | Jeremiah 31:31-33
 | I Corinthians 6:20
 | I John 3:1-2

Footnote 9 | Deuteronomy 6:4-5
 | Matthew 16:24-26
 | Mark 12:29-30

Footnote 10 | Psalm 24:1
 | John 1:1-4
 | Colossians 1:16-17

Gail P. Miller

Chapter Three
Why Do You Reject Me?

Why do **you** reject **Me**? Is it because of **your** pain and hurt? Why do **you** push **Me** away?
Is it because **you** think **I** would treat **you** like everyone else?

Why…**do you** run from **Me**?
Why…**do you** play games with **Me**?
Why…**do you** pretend with **Me**?
Why…**do you** resist **M***e?*
Why…**do you** try to hide from **Me**?
Why…**do you** use **Me** to make yourself look good?
Why…**do you** go without **Me***?*
Why…**do you** try to manipulate **Me**?
Why…**do you** lie to **Me**?
Why…**do you** leave **Me**?
Why…do you do these things to **Me?**[11]

True Love Has a Passion for You!

Don't **you** know...
        I AM...
              <u>the only one</u>
                      Who can *help* **you**?

Don't **you** know...
        I AM...
              <u>the only one</u>
                      Who can *heal* **you**?

Don't **you** know...
        I AM...
              <u>the only one</u>
                      Who can *deliver* **you**?

Don't **you** know...
        I AM...
              <u>the only one</u>
                      Who can *free* **you**?

Don't **you** know...
        I AM...
              <u>the only one</u>
                      Who can *promote* **you**?

Don't **you** know...
        I AM...
              <u>the only one</u>
                      Who can *feed* **you**?

Don't **you** know...
        I AM...
              <u>the only one</u>
                      Who can *keep* **you**?

Don't **you** know...
        I AM...
              <u>the only one</u>
                      Who can *lift* **you**?

Don't **you** know...
        I AM...
              <u>the only one</u>
                      Who can *save* **you**?

Don't **you** know…
        I AM…
                <u>the only one</u>
                        Who *knows* **you**?

Don't **you** know…
        I AM…
                <u>the only one</u>
                        Who can *reach* **you**?

Don't **you** know…
        I AM…
                <u>the only one</u>
                        Who *prepared* a place for **you**?

Don't **you** know…
        I AM…
                <u>the only one</u>
                        Who can *fulfill* **you**?

Don't **you** know…
        I AM…
                <u>the only one</u>
                        Who can make **you** *whole*?

Didn't **you** know?[12]

What really is the ***problem***?

Are *you* <u>afraid</u> I will reject **you**?[13]

True Love Has a Passion for You!

Scripture Reference

Footnote 11   Genesis 1:26-27
                     Romans 10:9-13
                     Ephesians 3:14-19

Footnote 12   Isaiah 53:5
                     Romans 5:6-8
                     Ephesians 1:3-8

Footnote 13   Psalm 103:1-5
                     Isaiah 45:19
                     I Peter 2:22-25

Gail P. Miller

Chapter Four
True Love Creates

The *reason* for the heavens and the earth is…
>because **I love you!**

The *reason* for day and night is…
>because **I love you!**

The *reason* for the sun and moon is…
>because **I love you!**

The *reason* for the stars and planets is…
>because **I love you!**

The *reason* for the plants and trees is…
>because **I love you!**

The *reason* for food and water is…
>because **I love you!**

The *reason* for the wind and rain is…
>because **I love you!**

The *reason* for seed time and harvest is…
>because **I love you!**

The *reason* for winter and summer is…
>because **I love you!**

The *reason* for spring and fall is…
>because **I love you!**

The *reason* for the birds and bees is…
>because **I love you!**

The *reason* for a man and a woman is…
>because **I love you!**

The *reason* for a father and a mother is…
>because **I love you!**

True Love Has a Passion for You!

The *reason* for a boy and a girl is...
                                         because **I love you!**

The *reason* for a father and a son is...
                                         because **I love you!**

The *reason* for a mother and a daughter is...
                                         because **I love you!**

The *reason* for creation is...
                                         because **I love you!**

The *reason* **I AM** here is...
                                         because **I love you!**

The *reason* is...
                                         I love you![14]

Gail P. Miller

To have **lived,**

died

and **not known** True Love

is…

a ***tragedy!***[15]

True Love Has a Passion for You!

Scripture Reference

Footnote 14	Genesis 1:1
	Genesis 8:22
	Colossians 1:16-18

Footnote 15	Deuteronomy 28:14
	Isaiah 29:13
	Matthew 7:21-23

Gail P. Miller

Chapter Five
Just Think!

Just think, all this time **you** were looking for **Me**, *I* was waiting for **you**. **You** have been looking for **Me** high and low, yet **I** have been right here all the time!

Think…
on the fact that
I want you!

Think…
on the fact that
I desire you!

Think…
on the fact that
I AM in love with you!

Think…
on the fact that
I long for you!

Think…
on the fact that
I came to you!

Think…
on the fact that
I look for you!

True Love Has a Passion for You!

Think…
on the fact that
I made a way for you!

Think…
on the fact that
I have a place for you!

Think…
on the fact that
I have plans for you!

Think…
on the fact that
I want to be pleased by you!

Think…
on the fact that
I AM… jealous over you!

Think…
on the fact that
I have blessings for you!

Think…
on the fact that
I have a purpose for you!

Think…
on the fact that
We will be together forever!

JUST THINK![16]

Gail P. Miller

Scripture Reference

Footnote 16

Exodus 34:1
Jeremiah 29:11-13
Philippians 4:7-8
Hebrews 11:5-6

True Love Has a Passion for You!

Chapter Six
What You Need is Me!

Let **Me** give **you** a taste of **Who I** really am. Are **you** ready? Then put this in **your** mouth and chew.

True Love includes everything. Nothing and no one is left out of True Love.

Whatever **you** should get out of a **husband**...
is in **Me**.

Whatever **you** should get out of a **wife**...
is in **Me**.

Whatever **you** should get out of a **son**...
is in **Me**.

Whatever **you** should get out of a **daughter**...
is in **Me**.

Whatever **you** should get out of a **father**...
is in **Me**.

Whatever **you** should get out of a **mother**...
is in **Me**.

True Love Has a Passion for You!

                                      Whatever **you** should get
              out of a **brother**…

is in **M***e.*

                                      Whatever **you** should get
              out of a **sister**…

is in **M***e.*

                                      Whatever **you** should get
              out of an **uncle**…

is in **M***e.*

                                      Whatever **you** should get
              out of an **aunt**…

is in **M***e.*

                                      Whatever **you** should get
              out of a **nephew**…

is in **M***e.*

                                      Whatever **you** should get
              out of a **niece**…

is in **M***e.*

                                      Whatever **you** should get
              out of a **cousin**…

is in **M***e.*

                                      Whatever **you** should get
              out of a **grandfather**…

is in **M***e.*

                                      Whatever **you** should get
              out of a **grandmother**…

is in **M***e.*

                                      Whatever **you** should get
              out of a **friend**…

is in **M***e.*

                                      Whatever **you** should get
              out of a **neighbor**…

is in **M***e.*

Gail P. Miller

                                      Whatever **you** should get
out of **food**…

is in **M***e.*

                                      Whatever **you** should get
out of **water**…

is in **M***e.*

                                      Whatever **you** should get
out of **rest**…

is in **M***e.*

                                      Whatever **you** should get
out of **exercise**…

is in **M***e.*

                                      Whatever **you** should get
out of **emotions**…

is in **M***e.*

                                      Whatever **you** should get
out of **knowledge**…

is in **M***e.*

                                      Whatever **you** should get
out of **understanding**…

is in **M***e.*

                                      Whatever **you** should get
out of **wisdom**…

is in **M***e.*

                                      Whatever **you** should get
out of **fame**…

is in **M***e.*

                                      Whatever **you** should get
out of **fortune**…

is in **M***e.*

                                      Whatever **you** should get
out of **sex**…

is in **M***e.*

True Love Has a Passion for You!

                                        Whatever **you** should get
              out of **alcohol**…

is in **M***e.*

                                        Whatever **you** should get
              out of **drugs**…

is in **M***e.*

                                        Whatever **you** should get
              out of **status**…

is in **M***e.*

                                        Whatever **you** should get
              out of **power**…

is in **M***e.*

                                        Whatever **you** should get
              out of **money**…

is in **M***e.*

                                        Whatever **you** should get
              out of **animals**…

is in **M***e.*

                                        Whatever **you** should get
            out of the **sun**…

is in **M***e.*

                                        Whatever **you** should get
            out of the **moon**…

is in **M***e.*

                                        Whatever **you** should get
            out of the **stars**…

is in **M***e.*

                                        Whatever **you** should get
            out of **life**…

is in **M***e.*

What *you* <u>need</u> is…

Me![17]

Gail P. Miller

Everything that

was,

is

and **shall be**

came out of

Me![18]

True Love Has a Passion for You!

Scripture Reference

Footnote 17

Psalm 34:8-9
II Corinthians 9:8
Colossians 1:16-17

Footnote 18

Deuteronomy 30:19-20
Joshua 24:15
John 3:16

Gail P. Miller

Chapter Seven
I Can't Choose for You!

You can choose to die or **you can choose to** live.
                                      I can't choose for you!
You can choose to be sad or **you can choose to** be glad.
                                      I can't choose for you!
You can choose to hold on to the pain or **you can choose to** let the pain go.   **I can't choose for you!**
You can choose to lie or **you can choose to** tell the truth.
                                      I can't choose for you!
You can choose to follow **your** flesh or **you can choose to** follow **your** heart.   **I can't choose for you!**
You can choose to worry or **you can choose to** have faith.
                                      I can't choose for you!
You can choose to doubt or **you can choose to** believe.
                                      I can't choose for you!
You can choose to hate or **you can choose to** live in peace.
                                      I can't choose for you!
You can choose to live in fear or **you can choose to** love.
                                      I can't choose for you!
You can choose to come or **you can choose to** go.
                                      I can't choose for you!
You can choose to blame or **you can choose to** forgive.
                                      I can't choose for you!
You can choose to tear down or **you can choose to** build up.
                                      I can't choose for you!

True Love Has a Passion for You!

You can choose to speak or **you can choose to** be silent.
                                        I can't choose for you!
You can choose to be poor in **Me** or **you can choose to** be rich in **Me**.
                                        I can't choose for you!
You can choose to disobey or **you can choose to** obey
                                        I can't choose for you!
You can choose against **Me** or **you can choose** in favor of **Me**.
                                        I can't choose for you!
You can choose to live without **Me** or **you can choose to** live with **Me**.

THE CHOICE IS YOURS![19]

Gail P. Miller

Scripture Reference

Footnote 19   Deuteronomy 30:19
                         Joshua 24:15
                         John 3:16

True Love Has a Passion for You!

Gail P. Miller

Chapter Eight
I Already Love You!

There's **one** thing **you** should know before **you** make **your** choice and that is, **I already love you!** [20]
        You don't have to have the finest clothes.
I already **love you!**
        You don't have to drive the fastest car.
I already **love you!**
        You don't have to be at the top of **your** class.
I already **love you!**
        You don't have to live in the biggest house.
I already **love you!**
        You don't have to be the richest of them all.
I already **love you!**
        You don't have to be handsome or pretty.
I already **love you!**
        You can be first or **you can be** last.
I already **love you!**
        You can be clothed or **you can be** naked.
I already **love you!**
        You can be walking, driving or **you can be** riding the bus.
I already **love you!**
        You can be making As and Bs or **you can be** making Ds and Fs.
I already **love you!**
        You can be a father or **you can be** fatherless.
I already **love you!**

True Love Has a Passion for You!

You can be a mother or you can be motherless.
I already love you!
You can be talented or you can have hidden talents.
I already love you!
You can have teeth or you can be toothless.
I already love you!
You can be young or you can be old.
I already love you!
You can be sick or you can be well.
I already love you!
You can have all of your body parts or you can have some of your body parts.
I already love you!
You can be employed or you can be unemployed.
I already love you!
You can be overweight or you can be underweight.
I already love you!
You can have the best of things or you can have the worst of things.
I already love you!
You can be succeeding or you can be failing in everything you do.
I already love you!
You can be an alcoholic or you can be sober.
I already love you!
You can be an addict or you can be delivered.
I already love you!
You can have a boyfriend or you can be without a boyfriend.
I already love you!
You can have a girlfriend or you can be without a girlfriend.
I already love you!
You can be married, divorced or you can be single.
I already love you!

You can be saved or **you can be** unsaved.

I already love you!

You can be in jail or **you can be** just released from jail.

I already love you!

You can be accepted by some or **you can be** rejected by others.

I already love you!

You don't have to prove <u>anything</u>.

You don't have to have <u>anything</u>.

You don't have to be <u>anything</u>.

I already love **you!**

I already love **you!**

I already love **you!**

YOU… ARE <u>ALREADY</u> LOVED![21]

True Love Has a Passion for You!

True Love is new everyday. Every day **you** will learn something new about **True Love**.

There is **security** in **True Love.**

There is a **place** to **hide.**

There is a **place** to **rest.**

True Love is perfect and perfect love removes all fears. Any fears that will keep **you** from receiving **Me**, **I** will get rid of them, because **nothing is impossible with True Love!**

I will never change.

I will never lie to **you**.

I will never leave **you**.

I will never break **My** promises to **you**.

I will never say, "I don't <u>love</u> **you** anymore!"

I will never be careless with the precious things **you** give **Me**.

I will never take back the gifts and callings **I** have given **you**.

I Am someone whom no one can ever take from you![22]

Gail P. Miller

I will show **you**
                My joy.

I will show **you**
                My peace.

I will show **you**
                My kindness.

I will show **you**
                My goodness.

I will show **you**
                My tenderness.

I will show **you**
                My correction.

because...discipline is...a part of love.

True Love Has a Passion for You!

You will find the comfort
                                   that **you** need.

You will find the rest
                                   that **you** need.

You will find the care
                                   that **you** need.

You will find the training
                                   that you need.

You will find…
                                   that **True Love**

makes an excellent place to <u>grow</u>.

Gail P. Miller

Did **you** ever hear of a game called, "He or she loves **Me**, he or she loves **Me** not?" Well, **I** say, no need to play games.

I LOVE YOU!

I have given you a taste of who **True Love** really is and **I** believe you will make your choice today. Today, you heard **True Love's** voice. **I** trust you will open your heart and believe what **I** have said. If you believe **My Word** to be true, just call out to **Me** and **I** will answer.

Remember, **I** can't choose for you because **True Love** allows you to choose. Therefore, all that **I** have said is to let you know this…

All I want is… YOU![23]

True Love Has a Passion for You!

Scripture Reference

Footnote 20　　　　　　　　Jeremiah 31:3
　　　　　　　　　　　　　John 3:16
　　　　　　　　　　　　　Romans 5:8

Footnote 21　　　　　　　　Psalm 91:1-2
　　　　　　　　　　　　　Proverbs 10:12
　　　　　　　　　　　　　Matthew 11:28-30

Footnote 22　　　　　　　　Romans 11:29
　　　　　　　　　　　　　Hebrews 6:18
　　　　　　　　　　　　　I Peter 5:7

Footnote 23　　　　　　　　Proverbs 22:6
　　　　　　　　　　　　　Galatians 5:22-23
　　　　　　　　　　　　　Revelations 3:20

Gail P. Miller

Prophetic Poetic Mysteries

True Love Has a Passion for You!

Gail P. Miller

Word of the Lord

True Love Has a Passion for You!

Word of the Lord!

"The effect of arrogance, Disrespect and Desire, for Gain." All three are offenses to **God**. All three are seated in **God's House**. Hear the **Word** of the **Lord**. (Deut. 8:11-14; 17-19; Job 27:13-19) (Eccles 2:26 –TANAKH)

> The **Word** of **Knowledge** given on 04/29/99 to Dr. Diane Parks-Love, from the Spirit of the **Lord**, describing the "Church" as a woman. It is a personification.

This is what the **Lord** says, "**My Church** has given herself to perform whoredoms with the world. She has taken the jewels (*Private Parts*) of her *Holiness* and profaned them, by joining with her lovers. **My** people (*Leaders*) have become her pimps for they have taken her out among the heathen and sold her for gain. The people of **God** have brought into her other lovers and they have opened her up and exposed her private parts, to sorcerers and demons. They have brought evil, satanic games to be played in **My House** and have brought entertainment before **My Altar** and played them in **My Face**."

"They have lessened the **Holiness of My Bride** and made her a whore, for she has compromised **My** love for her and taken the secrets of our union and the intimacy of our "*bedchamber*" and mingled these precious secrets with strange lovers."

"She is diseased and filthy with infections. **My** wrath and indignation has risen from **My Holy Place** and I have come out against her. She will continue to feel the effects of **My Wrath**, until **I** have fulfilled **My Judgments** against her faithlessness and cleansed her. Men will continue to come into her, believing they can mingle their profanities with **My Wife** but **I** will destroy them. They will continue to die in her presence and to her shame, until she repents and turns back to her **Husband**."

"For **I AM** the **Lord** and there is none other beside **Me**. **I** will purify **My Bed Chamber** and once again, **I** will make love to **My Wife** and she will again know the ecstasy that is **Mine** alone to give. As **I** came down in the *Garden* to her, so **I** will come again to her, for she will be **Mine**. **I** will cleanse *Her*!"

True Love Has a Passion for You!

Whose House is It Anyway?

You make decisions on
        who should preach in
                My House.

You make decisions on
        who should come forth in
                My House.

You make decisions on
        the limits of **My** people in
                My House.

You make decisions on
        the gifts and callings of **My** daughters in
                My House.

You make decisions on
        how to worship **Me** in
                My House.

You make decisions on
        the order of service in
                My House.

You make decisions on
        how **you** should praise **Me** in
                My House.

You make decisions on
        who will shepherd **My** flock by voting in
                My House.

Gail P. Miller

You make decisions on
> having programs to take up offerings in
>> **My** House.

You make decisions on
> having concerts in
>> **My** House.

You make decisions on
> selling **your** wares in
>> **My** House.

You make decisions on
> how things should run in
>> **My** House.

You make decisions on
> yoking **yourselves** up with the world in
>> **My** House.

You make decisions on
> your own teachings and belief systems in
>> **My** House.

<u>**Isn't it written?**</u> "Therefore He says:
When He ascended on high, He led captivity
captive, and gave gifts to men."
—Ephesians 4:8

<u>**Isn't it written?**</u> "Then He taught, saying to them, "Is it
not written, 'My house shall be called a house of
prayer for all nations'? But you have made it a
den of thieves."
—Mark 11:17

<u>**Isn't it written?**</u> "But the hour is coming, and now is
when the true worshippers will worship the
Father in spirit and truth; for the Father is seeking

True Love Has a Passion for You!

such to worship Him. God *is* Spirit, and those who worship Him must worship in spirit and **truth**."
—John 4:23-24

Isn't it written? "And it shall come to pass in the last days, says God, that I will pour out My Spirit on all flesh; your sons and your daughters shall prophesy, your young men shall see visions, your old men shall dream dreams. And on My menservants and on My maidservants I will pour out My Spirit in those days; and they shall prophesy."
—Acts 2:17-18

Isn't it written? "Adulterers and adulteresses! Do you not know that friendship with the world is enmity with God? Whoever therefore wants to be a friend of the world makes himself an enemy of God."
—James 4:4

Isn't it written? "The earth is the Lord's, and all its fullness, the world and those who dwell therein."
—Psalm 24:1

Isn't it written? "Where were you when I laid the foundations of the earth? Tell *Me*, if you have understanding."
—Job 38:4

So...**Whose** house is it anyway?

Gail P. Miller

I Don't Know You!

Surely, I got saved years ago when someone witnessed to me. I have been saved from a child. I am saved. I got saved when I heard about **You** in a meeting.

"But **I** don't <u>know</u> **you!**"

Surely, I come to church three times a week for prayer and on Sunday. I come to bible study. I come to youth meetings, board meetings, vacation bible school and other meetings.

"But **I** don't <u>know</u> **you!**"

Surely, I am on the deacon board, I am an usher. I sing in the choir, I am a youth pastor, a Sunday school teacher, I am the secretary at my church and I help in the kitchen. I sit on the fourth row from the back on the left side. My family founded this church.

"But **I** don't <u>know</u> **you!**"

Surely, I pray to **you** each morning and night, witness to people, lay hands on the sick, cast out demons and thousands get saved in my meetings each week. Last year alone more people got saved in my meetings than in any other meetings and I have the numbers to prove it.

"But **I** don't <u>know</u> **you!**"

Surely, I asked **You** for a wife/husband and **You** gave them to me. I asked for a house, a car, job, building, money, friends, ministry, parents, etc. and I pay my tithes and offerings every week.

"**You** know, satan gives gifts too!"

Surely, I have built one of the largest churches on record, TV stations, radio stations, made movies, cut CDs, won many awards, had songs on the charts, record deals, I have written songs, books and been on TV shows. I was asked to come and preach for so and so; I turned the house out and got a standing ovation.

True Love Has a Passion for You!

"But **I** don't <u>know</u> **you**!"

Surely, I travel all over the country and the world. They call me to take up offerings. They say I am on the cutting edge as a minister. I have over 10,000 members, or I have few members. I have the biggest bible study in the city or the smallest. I have partners from all over the world who support my ministry. I am on the internet with a website and I share excerpts of my messages. People can download my sermons or songs onto an I-pod to carry them around.

"But **I** don't <u>know</u> **you**!"

Surely, I don't drink or smoke. I have not fornicated. I don't go to clubs or I don't go to clubs anymore. I don't dance or wear clothes that expose me. I have been faithful to **You** and my church. I have always wanted to preach, teach, evangelize or do something for **You** since I was little. I have been in the church all my life or I have not been in the church all my life.

"But **I** don't <u>know</u> **you**!"

Surely, all these things I have asked and done by faith. I stood and did not waiver. I speak with tongues of men and the angelic host. I have the gifts of prophecy, understand all mysteries and **You** gave me knowledge. My faith is so strong that I can remove mountains. I have distributed all my produce to feed the poor and granted **You** my body to be put to the fire.

"And, it still has not profited **you** anything."

What? I did all these things for **You**; I followed **Your Word**. I read **Your Word**. I studied **Your Word**. I obeyed **Your Word** to the best of my knowledge. I treated my wife/husband, family, friends, neighbors, co-workers and my boss right. I have kept the integrity of

Gail P. Miller

my ministry and I have or have not gone to the ends of the earth with **Your** message. How can they hear unless someone is sent? So I went. I did everything **You** asked me to, to the letter.

Hear the **Word** of the **Lord**!

"**I still** don't <u>know</u> **you**!"

Proverbs 14:12
Matthew 7:21-23
I Corinthians 9:27
I Corinthians 13:1-3
II Corinthians 3:6

True Love Has a Passion for You!

Alliances!

"Can two walk together, unless they are agreed?"
—Amos 3:3

"Do not be deceived: "Evil company corrupts good habits."
—I Corinthians 15:33

"Do not be unequally yoked together with unbelievers. For what fellowship has righteousness with lawlessness? And what communion has light with darkness? And what accord has Christ with Belial? Or what part has a believer with and unbeliever?
And what agreement has the temple of God with idols? For you are the temple of the living God."
—II Corinthians 6:14-16

"Adulterers and adulteresses! Do you not know that friendship with the world is enmity with God? Whoever therefore wants to be a friend of the world makes himself an enemy of God."
—James 4:4

"Thus says the Lord:
'Cursed is the man who trust in man
And makes flesh his strength,
Whose heart departs form the Lord'"
—Jeremiah 17:5

Gail P. Miller

"Unless the Lord builds the house,
They labor in vain who build it;
Unless the Lord guards the city,
The watchman stay awake in vain."
—Psalm 127:1

"He who has an ear, let him hear what
the Spirit says to the churches."
—Revelation 2:29

True Love Has a Passion for You!

I Don't Need!

I don't <u>need</u> a feather, quill, pen, pencil or
a piece of paper to declare **My** message.

I can speak for **Myself**!

I don't <u>need</u> a drum, a smoke signal, town crier,
telegram or pony express to declare **My** message.

I can speak for **Myself**!

I don't <u>need</u> Morris code, sonar, radar or the
Dewy Decimal System to declare **My** message.

I can speak for **Myself**!

I don't <u>need</u> a radio, TV, CB or a
walkie talkie to declare **My** message.

I can speak for **Myself**!

I don't <u>need</u> a letter, postcard, e-mail, magazine
or a newspaper to declare **My** message.

I can speak for **Myself**!

I don't <u>need</u> a mail-carrier, special delivery, air-mail
or over night services to declare **My** message.

I can speak for **Myself**!

I don't <u>need</u> a landline, cell phone, printer
or a fax machine to declare **My** message.

Gail P. Miller

I can speak for **Myself**!

I don't <u>need</u> a siren; an emergency broadcast system, amber alert or news caster to declare **My** message.

I can speak for **Myself**!

I don't need a computer, I-pod, I-pad, notebook, tablet, lap-top, VCR, CD, DVD, MP3, record player, app, social media, or any other kind of device to declare **My** message.

I can speak for **Myself**!

I don't <u>need</u> a cable, a dish, a receiver or a satellite to declare **My** message.

I can speak for **Myself**!

I don't <u>need</u> an instrument, a tool, a person or a thing to declare **My** *own* message.

It just pleases **Me** to do so.

In the beginning, **I** said, "Let there be…" and there was.

I AM Communication!

Genesis 1:1-26
Isaiah 40:28
John 1:1-4
Romans 11:33
Colossians 1:16-17
Revelation 1:7

True Love Has a Passion for You!

Consider This!

"But if you do not forgive, neither will
your Father in heaven forgive your trespasses."
—Mark 11:26

"But you are not in the flesh but in the
Spirit, if indeed the Spirit of God dwells in
you. Now if anyone does not have the Spirit
of Christ, he is not His." —Romans 8:9

"But in a great house there are not only
vessels of gold and silver, but also of wood
and clay, some for honor and some for dishonor."
—II Timothy 2:20

"But if you are without chastening of
which all have become partakers, then you
are illegitimate and not sons." —Hebrews 12:8

"If anyone defiles the temple of God,
God will destroy him. For the temple of
God is holy, which *temple* you are." —I Corinthians 3:17

"If anyone does not abide in Me, he is
cast out as a branch and is withered; and
they gather them and throw *them* into the
fire, and they are burned." —John 15:6

"For if we sin willfully after we have
received the knowledge of truth, there
no longer remains a sacrifice for sins." —Hebrews 10:26

Gail P. Miller

"For the wages of sin *is* death, but the
Gift of God *is* eternal life in Christ Jesus
our Lord." —Romans 6:23

"But if you have bitter envy and self-
seeking in your heart, do not boast and
lie against the truth.
This wisdom does not descend from
above, but *is* earthly, **sensual**, demonic.
For where envy and self-seeking *exist*,
Confusion and every evil thing *are* there." —James 3:14-16

"And then I will declare to them I
never knew you; depart from Me, you who
practice lawlessness!" —Matthew 7:21-23

"Hear **The Word** of the **Lord**."
"Now is the time to consider **My** ifs, ands, fors or buts."
—Psalm 95:7-8; Hebrews 3:7-8

True Love Has a Passion for You!

My Holiness

My Name is in **you,**
My Spirit is in **you,**
My Power is in **you,**
My Glory is in **you,**
My Honor is in **you,**
My Majesty is in **you,**
My Tabernacle is in **you,**
My Unmatchable Fame is in **you.**

"If anyone defiles the temple of God, God will destroy him. For the temple of God is holy, which *temple* you are."

I must protect **My Holiness!**

Leviticus 10:3
I Corinthians 3:17
Hebrews 3:7-8

Gail P. Miller

Intimacy with God!

So… that the work **you** do
will be the work that **I** planned
instead of the work that
you do…
for **Me!**

Luke 6:46-49
Matthew 7:21-23

True Love Has a Passion for You!

Word of the Lord!

You cannot be whole until
you are willing to be honest
with **Me**!

I want **you** to be **My** friend.

You think you have time;
I Am…time!

Exodus 3:14
Psalm 103:1-5
Proverbs 18:24
I John 1:5-10

Gail P. Miller

Word of the Lord!

I AM Truth
I AM Faith
I AM Wisdom
I AM Knowledge
I AM Understanding
I AM Counsel
I AM Might
I AM Holy
I AM Righteousness
I AM the perfect and only **"Measuring Stick"** of right.
Therefore, whatever **I** say is…
Holiness!

John 14:6
Leviticus 11:44-45
I Peter 1:16
Deuteronomy 8:3
Matthew 4:4
Isaiah 11:2
Deuteronomy 6:4
Mark 12:29
Exodus 3:14

True Love Has a Passion for You!

Word of the Lord!

"Those of **you** who are lifted up by the world, when **you** get saved… **you** do not make a lateral move from the kingdom of darkness to the kingdom of light."

"Everyone starts at the foot of the cross where the ground is level!"

I Corinthians 12:13
Galatians 3:26-28
I Timothy 3:1-7

Gail P. Miller

Word of the Lord!

You go to work
to make a living,
but **you** are missing life
so that **you** <u>can</u> live*!*

Acts 2:42
Romans 13:11
Hebrews 10:25

True Love Has a Passion for You!

Word of the Lord

Who is the church?
Is it the bricks?
Is it the stick?
Is it the mortar?
You have built the wrong church debt free.
You need to repent and seek **Me**!

Acts 20:28
Colossians 1:24
I Corinthians 3:17

Gail P. Miller

Do You Love Me My Way?

"If you love Me, keep My commandments."
"Do **you** love **Me, My** way?"

"If anyone
desires to come after Me, let him deny
himself, and take up his cross daily, and
follow Me."
"Do **you** love **Me My** way?"

"For whoever desires to save his life
will lose it, but whoever loses his life for My
sake and the gospel's will save it."
"Do **you** love **Me My** way?"

"If anyone defiles the temple of God,
God will destroy him. For the temple of
God is holy, which *temple* you are."
"Do **you** love **Me My** way?"

If someone says, "I love God," and
hates his brother, he is a liar; for he who does
not love his brother whom he has seen, how
can he love God whom he has not seen?
"Do **you** love **Me My** way?"

"For if you forgive men their trespasses,
your heavenly Father will also forgive you.
But if you do not forgive men their
trespasses, neither will your Father forgive
your trespasses."
"Do **you** love **Me My** way?"

True Love Has a Passion for You!

"For My thoughts *are* not your thoughts,
Nor *are* your ways My ways," says the Lord.

"For as the heavens are higher than
the earth,
So are My ways higher than your ways,
And My thoughts than your thoughts."

"Do **you** love **Me My** way?"

"Yes, **I** love **you** but,
Do **you** love **Me** back **My** way?"

John 14:15
Luke 9:23
Mark 8:35
I Corinthians 3:17
I John 4:20
Matthew 6:14-15
Isaiah 55:8-9

Gail P. Miller

When It's Time, I Will Bring It to Pass!

"To everything *there is* a season,
A time for every purpose under heaven:
A time to be born
And a time to die;
A time to plant,
And a time to pluck *what* is planted;"

"When it's time, **I will bring it to pass.**"

"A time to kill,
And a time to heal;
A time to break down,
And a time to build up;"

"When it's time, **I will bring it to pass.**"

"A time to weep,
And a time to **laugh**;
A time to mourn,
And a time to dance;"

"When it's time, **I will bring it to pass.**"

"A time to cast away stones,
And a time to gather stones;
A time to embrace,
And time to refrain from embracing;"

True Love Has a Passion for You!

"When it's time, **I will bring it to pass.**"

"A time to gain,
And a time to lose;
A time to keep,
And a time to throw away;"

"When it's time, **I will bring it to pass.**"

"A time to tear,
And a time to sew;
A time to keep silence,
And a time to speak;"

"When it's time, **I will bring it to pass.**"

"A time to love,
And a time to hate;
A time of war,
And a time of peace,"

"When it's time, **I will bring it to pass.**"

"I know that whatever God does,
It shall be forever.
Nothing can be added to it,
And nothing taken from it.
God does *it*, that men should fear
before Him."

Gail P. Miller

"That which is has already been,
And what is to be has already been;
And God requires an account of
what is past."

Why?

I AM...time!

>Ecclesiastes 3:1-8
>Ecclesiastes 3:14-15

True Love Has a Passion for You!

Cry Out to Me!

Cry out to **Me**
For **your** garments are moth eaten.
—Job 13:28

Cry out to **Me**
For **your** souls suffer leanness.
—Psalm 106:15, Isaiah 10:16

Cry out to **Me**
For **you** are like white washed tombs.
—Matthew 23:27, Acts 23:3a

Cry out to **Me**
For **you** are full of dead men's bones, all uncleanness, hypocrisy and lawlessness.
—Matthew 23:27-28

Cry out to **Me**
For **you** are an adulteress woman.
—Proverbs 30:20, Hosea 2:2-5

Cry out to **Me**
For **your** whoredoms have come up before me.
—Ezekiel 16:20, 22, 25, 28, 34-36; Hosea 4:12, 5:4

Cry out to **Me**
For **you** are the church and judgment starts in My house!
—James 3:1; I Peter 4:17

True Love Has a Passion for You!

Seek Me to Find Out Who You Are!

"A man's steps are of the Lord;
How then can a man understand his
own way?"

"**Call** to Me, and I will answer you, and
show you great and mighty things, which
you do not know."

"So I say to you, 'Ask, and it will be
given to you; seek, and you will find;
knock, and it will be opened to you.
For everyone who asks receives, and
he who seeks, finds, and to him who knocks
it will be opened.'"

"If you then, being evil, know how to
give good gifts, to your children, how much
more will *your* heavenly Father give the
Holy Spirit to those who ask Him!"

"However, when He, the Spirit of truth
has come, He will guide you into all truth;
for He will not speak on His own *authority*,
but what ever He hears He will speak; and
He will tell you things to come."

"Likewise the Spirit also helps in our weaknesses. For we do not know what we should pray for as we ought, but the Spirit Himself makes intercession for us with groanings which cannot be uttered."

"Now He who searches the hearts knows what the mind of the Spirit *is*, because he makes intercession for the saints according to the *will* of God."

"The steps of a *good* man are ordered by the Lord, And He delights in his way."

"Therefore, seek **Me** to find out who **you** are,

In Me!"

Proverbs 20:24
Jeremiah 33:3
Luke 11:9-10, 13
John 16:13
Romans 8:26-27
Psalm 37:23

True Love Has a Passion for You!

I Own It All

Heaven and earth
I own them.
Houses and lands
I own them.
Money and things
I own them.
Places and people
I own them.
Systems and time
I control them.
Fame and fortune
I give them.
Relationships and family
I Am them.
So... what did **I** die to give **you**?
To <u>know</u> **Me!**

Psalm 24:1
John 10:10
John 17:2-3

Gail P. Miller

My Heart Aches!

When **you** depend upon people
instead of **Me**,
> **My** heart aches.

When **you** choose another relationship
over **Me**,
> **My** heart aches

When **you** spend more time with someone or something
rather than **Me**,
> **My** heart aches.

When **you** preach and teach about **Me**
and **you** don't even know **Me**,
> **My** heart aches.

When **you** spend your time thinking about other things
rather than **Me**,
> **My** heart aches.

When **you** as a body, operate in division and come
against **Me**,
> **My** heart aches.

When **you**, **My** children, live in sin,
> **My** heart aches.

I AM in pain!

> Genesis 6:6
> I Samuel 8:7-8
> II Chronicles 24:20
> Mark 3:5
> Luke 13:34
> Ephesians 4:30

True Love Has a Passion for You!

Give Me a Chance!

Give **Me** a chance to
Talk to **you**.

Give **Me** a chance to
Be with **you**.

Give **Me** a chance to
Draw close to **you**.

Give **Me** a chance to
Sit with **you**.

Give **Me** a chance to
Touch **you**.

Give **Me** a chance to
Take care of **you**.

Give **Me** a chance to
Be intimate with **you**.

Give **Me** the chance that
you gave others.

Just, Give **Me** that Chance!

Proverbs 17:17a
Proverbs 18:24
John 15:9-14

Gail P. Miller

Bring Me Your Heart!

Bring **Me your** heart.
Bring **Me your** heart.
Bring **Me your** heart and <u>lay</u> it before **Me**.

Bring **Me your** heart.
Bring **Me your** heart.
Bring **Me your** heart for it is the place of **My** <u>testing</u>.

Bring **Me your** heart.
Bring **Me your** heart.
Bring **Me your** heart for it is where **I** hide **My** <u>treasure</u>.

Bring **Me your** heart.
Bring **Me your** heart.
Bring **Me your** heart for it is where **I** come to <u>fellowship</u>.

Bring **Me your** heart!
Bring **Me your** heart!
For that's where **I** will place **My** <u>Son</u>!

Deuteronomy 8:2
Isaiah 29:13
Luke 17:21
Romans 10:9-13
II Corinthians 4:7

True Love Has a Passion for You!

Come Rest

Come *rest* within **My Bosom**.
Come *rest* with **your Father**.
Come *rest* with **your Friend**.
Come *rest* with **your Lover**.
Come *rest* with **My Spirit**.
Come lay with **Me**
and *rest*!

Psalm 37:7
Matthew 11:29-30
Hebrews 4:9-11

Gail P. Miller

Freely!

You can eat freely from
The Tree of Life.

You can eat freely of
the fruit of **The True Vine**.

You can drink freely from
the well of **Living Water**.

You can take all **you**
want from **My** banquet table.

Just… do it **Freely!**

Genesis 2:16
Matthew 10:8
Revelation 21:6
Revelation 22:17

True Love Has a Passion for You!

No Matter What!

NO MATTER WHAT **YOU'VE** DONE,
MY LOVE FOR **YOU** IS STILL THE SAME!

NO MATTER WHERE **YOU'VE** BEEN,
MY LOVE FOR **YOU** IS STILL THE SAME!

NO MATTER WHAT **YOU'VE** SAID,
MY LOVE FOR **YOU** IS STILL THE SAME!

NO MATTER WHO **YOU'VE** BEEN WITH,
MY LOVE FOR **YOU** IS STILL THE SAME!

NO MATTER WHO **YOU** WERE BORN TO,
MY LOVE FOR **YOU** IS STILL THE SAME!

SAVED OR NOT, IT DOESN'T MATTER,
MY LOVE FOR **YOU** IS STILL THE SAME!

EVEN **YOU**, IT DOESN'T MATTER,
MY LOVE FOR **YOU** IS STILL THE SAME!

IT DOESN'T MATTER,
MY LOVE IS THE SAME STILL… FOR **YOU**!

Romans 5:8
John 3:16
John 15:13-14

Gail P. Miller

I Just Wanted to Say

I just wanted to say,

"How are **you**?"

I just wanted to say,

"I miss **you**!"

I just wanted to say,

"I love **you**!"

I just wanted to say,

"Where are **you**?"

I... needed to say!!!

Genesis 3:9
John 3:16
John 17:8, 23, 26
Ephesians 1:3-6

True Love Has a Passion for You!

Dwelling Place

I AM looking for a **Tabernacle.**
I AM looking for a **Sanctuary.**
I AM looking for a **Temple.**
I AM looking for a **House.**
I AM looking for a **City.**
I AM looking for a **Garden.**
I AM looking
I AM looking
I AM looking
at
You!

John 4:23-24
I Corinthians 6:19-20

Gail P. Miller

Those Same People!

Those same people... who cheered and said Hosanna when **I** road in to town on the donkey, cried crucify **Him**.

Those same people... who came to hear **Me** teach and eat the food **I** blessed, kicked and spit on **Me**.

Those same people... who said they loved **Me**, turned their backs on **Me**.

Those same people... who followed after **Me** and sought **Me** out, walked away from **Me** never to be seen with **Me** again.

Those same people... who ate with **Me** and stayed with **Me**, persecuted **Me**.

Those same people... who saw and experienced **My** miracles, don't believe in **Me** anymore.

Those same people... who **I** set free from demons are now bound again.

Those same people... who say they know **Me** and **My Word**, live in doubt and fear.

True Love Has a Passion for You!

Those same people… who were on fire for **Me** are now lukewarm.

Those same people… who said they would die for **Me**, denied **Me** before men.

Those same people… who said they could not live without **Me**, have gone and walked their own way.

Those same people… who walked with **Me** to the cross, beat **Me**, cast lots for **My** garments and pierced **Me** in **My** side!

But, **I** still died for… those same people!

Acts 3:17
Luke 23:34

Gail P. Miller

Songs of the *Lord*

&

Songs of Gail

True Love Has a Passion for You!

Broken by the Lord
(Song of the Gail)

We are broken by the **Lord**
We are broken by the **Lord**

From our vessels, seeps **His Oil**.
From our cracks, flows **His Love**.
From our pieces, **His Glory** is seen.

Yes, yes, yes, yes we are broken for the **Lord**.

Chorus: We are broken by the **Lord**,
        We are broken by the **Lord**,
        Broken, broken, broken, we are broken for the **Lord**.

Vamp: Like a clay pot on a potter's wheel,
        You are broken into pieces.
        You are shattered for **His** praise,
        Recreated for **His** pleasure.
        Broken, broken, broken, we are broken for the **Lord**.

Chorus: Repeat

Verse: Out of **your** being, comes **His** plan.
       Out of **your** mind, flows understanding.
       Out of **your** heart, pours **His** perfect will.
       If **you** are willing then, come…come…come and be broken by the **Lord**.

Jeremiah 18:1-6
Matthew 21:44
Luke 20:18

Gail P. Miller

Sing Songs
(Song of Gail)

Sing songs
Sing songs
Make melody in **your** heart to **Him.**

Sing songs
Sing songs
Make melody in **your** heart to **Him.**

Sing songs
Sing songs
Make melody in **your** heart to **Him.**

Sing songs
Sing songs
from **your** heart to **Him.**

Sing songs
Sing songs
Make melody in **your** heart to **Him.**

Sing songs
Sing songs
from **your** heart to **Him.**

Acts 16:25
Ephesians 5:19
James 5:13

True Love Has a Passion for You!

Great Joy!
(Song of the **Lord**)

Great joy in the city
Great joy in the city
Great joy in the city
There's great joy to the **Lord**

Great joy in the city
Great joy in the city
Great joy in the city
And it's heard from miles around

Great joy in the city
There's great joy in the city
Great joy in the city
And it's heard from miles around

Great joy
Great joy
Great joy
Great joy
Great joy… in the city!

Psalm 100: 1-5
Psalm 98:1-9
Matthew 7:14

Gail P. Miller

Let Him Have His Way!
(Song of Gail)

Let **Him** have **His** way
in **your** praise.

Let **Him** have **His** way
in **your** worship.

Let **Him** have **His** way
in **your** song.

Let **Him** have **His** way
in **your** dance.

<u>Chorus</u>
Let **Him** have **His** way
Let **Him** have **His** way
Let **Him** have **His** way in **you**

Let **Him** have **His** way
Let **Him** have **His** way
Let **Him** have **His** way in **you**

Psalm 37:5
John 14:6

True Love Has a Passion for You!

The Lord by His Spirit is Moving!
(Song of the Gail)

The **Lord** by **His Spirit** is moving.
The **Lord** by **His Spirit** is moving.
The **Lord** by **His Spirit** is moving all over the plant earth!

The **Lord** by **His Spirit** is moving.
The **Lord** by **His Spirit** is moving.
The **Lord** by **His Spirit** is moving throughout the heavens above!

The **Lord** by **His Spirit** is moving.
The **Lord** by **His Spirit** is moving.
The **Lord** by **His Spirit** is moving on the face of the deep!

The **Lord** by **His Spirit** is moving.
The **Lord** by **His Spirit** is moving.
The **Lord** by **His Spirit** is moving among **His** chosen people!

The **Lord** by **His Spirit** is moving.
The **Lord** by **His Spirit** is moving.
The **Lord** by **His Spirit** is moving on your sons and daughters!

The **Lord** by **His Spirit** is moving.
The **Lord** by **His Spirit** is moving.
The **Lord** by **His Spirit** is moving to save the sin sick soul!

Gail P. Miller

"And, it shall come to pass in the last days," says God, "that I will pour out My Spirit on all flesh."

The **Lord**, by **His Spirit**… is moving!

Joel 2:28-29
Acts 2:17-18

True Love Has a Passion for You!

The Daughters of the Lord!
(Song of the **Lord**)

Here they come; the daughters of the **Lord.**
Here they come; the daughters of the **Lord.**
Here they come; the daughters of the **Lord**
to declare the power of **My Name**!

Here they come; the daughters of the **Lord.**
Here they come; the daughters of the **Lord.**
Here they come; the daughters of the **Lord**
to proclaim **Me, Oh Most High**!

Here they come; the daughters of the **Lord.**
Here they come; the daughters of the **Lord.**
Here they come; the daughters of the **Lord**
to reveal **My Matchless Fame!**

<u>Chorus</u>
Here they come
Here they come
Here they come; the daughters of **Lord**
to do great exploits.

Numbers 27:1-8
Daniel 11:32
Acts 2:17-18

Gail P. Miller

She Speaks
(Song of the **Lord**)

She speaks, in her ancient tongues, the great mysteries of **I AM**!

She speaks, in her native language, the praise and glory that is due **Me**!

She speaks, in her original vernacular, the clarity of **My Word**.

She speaks!

Judges 5:1-31
Acts 2:17-18

True Love Has a Passion for You!

Love is Stronger!
(Song of the **Lord**)

Love is stronger
Love is stronger
Love is stronger than death
That's why… no weapon formed against **Love** can bring death any triumph.

Love is stronger
Love is stronger
Love is stronger than death
That's why… no weapon formed against **Love** can bring death any celebration.

Love is stronger
Love is stronger
Love is stronger than death
That's why… no weapon formed against **Love** can bring death any jubilee.

Love is stronger
Love is stronger
Love is stronger than death
That's why… no weapon formed against **Love** can bring death any victory.

Love is stronger
Love is stronger
Love is stronger than death
That's why… no weapon formed against **Love** can bring death any praise.

Gail P. Miller

Love is stronger
Love is stronger
Love is stronger than death
That's why… no weapon formed against **Love** can bring death any power.

Love is stronger
Love is stronger
Love is stronger than death
Therefore… no weapon formed against **Love** will ever be able to prosper.

Song of Solomon 8:6-7
I Corinthians 13:8
I Corinthians 15:27

True Love Has a Passion for You!

Healing is the Children's Bread
(Song of the **Lord**)

Healing is the children's bread.

Healing is the children's bread.

Healing is the children's bread

and **Christ** has kept **you** fed.

Why? Because **Christ** is that **Bread!**

John 6:41, 48
Matthew 4:4
Mark 7:27

Gail P. Miller

Only You!
(Song of Gail)

Only **Christ** could die on the cross for **you**.

Only **You, Lord,** only **You!**

Only **Christ** could take away **your** sin.

Only **You, Lord,** only **You!**

Only **Christ** could save **your** soul from hell!

Only **You, Lord**, only **You!**

Only **Christ** could call **you** out of darkness.

Only **You, Lord**, only **You!**

Only **Christ** could make **you** holy like **I AM**.

<u>Chorus</u>

Only **You, Lord**, only **You!**

Only **You,**

Only **You,**

Only **You, Lord**, only… **You!**

John 1:29
John 3:16-17
Acts 2:38

True Love Has a Passion for You!

Open Your Heart!
(Song of Gail)

Open **your** heart and
Let **Him** in.
He can be trusted with the things within.

Open **your** heart and
Let **Him** in.

Open **your** heart and
Let **Him** in.
He can be trusted to work from within.
His power is real and **His** love is true, so

Open **your** heart and
Let **Him** in.

Open **your** heart and
Let **Him** in
to penetrate **your** heart so **He** can sing from within.

Open **your** heart and
Let **Him** in.

Open **your** heart and
Let **Him** in.
He's the one designed to fit from within.

Gail P. Miller

Open **your** heart
Open **your** heart
Open wide **your** heart and let **your True Lover** in.

He's knocking!

Romans 10:9-10
Hebrews 4:7

True Love Has a Passion for You!

How Great is Our God?
(Song of Gail)

How great
How great
How great is **our God?**

How great
How great
How great is **our God?**

He is greater
He is greater
He is greater than **you'll** ever know!

He is greater
He is greater
He is greater than **you'll** ever know!

Psalm 145:3
Romans 11:33

Gail P. Miller

Sing to the Lord!
(Song of Gail)

Sing of **His Grace**
Sing of **His Grace**
He gave **you** a voice to sing of **His Grace**.

Sing **His Praise**
Sing **His Praise**
He gave **you** a voice to sing **His Praise**.

Sing of **His Glory**
Sing of **His Glory**
He gave **you** a voice to sing of **His Glory**.

Sing of **His Honor**
Sing of **His Honor**
He gave **you** a voice to sing of **His Honor**.

Sing of **His Power**
Sing of **His Power**
He gave **you** a voice to sing of **His Power**.

<u>Chorus</u>
Sing to the **Lord**
Sing to the **Lord**
Sing and declare **His Name**.

True Love Has a Passion for You!

Sing to the **Lord**
Sing to the **Lord**
That's why **you** were created… to sing to the **Lord**!

Psalm 98:1-9
Psalm 100:1-5
James 5:13

Gail P. Miller

Stand in the Name of Jesus
(Song of Gail)

Chorus
Stand in the name of **Jesus** stand.
Stand when satan tempts **you** stand.
Jesus shed **His** blood for **you** so live the life **He** gave to **you.**
Stand, stand, just stand.

Verse
Even though the storms are ragging
and the winds are blowing just stand, stand.
Having the whole armor of **God** always on you
using the weapon of the **Word**.

Chorus
Stand in the name of **Jesus** stand.
Stand when satan tempts **you** stand.
Jesus shed **His** blood for **you** so, live the life he gave to **you**
Stand, stand, just stand.
Stand, stand, just stand.
Stand, stand, just stand.

Isaiah 59:19
Ephesians 6:11-18
James 4:6-7

True Love Has a Passion for You!

God and You!
(Song of Gail)

God and **you**
God and **you**
This is what **He** wants just,
God and **you**!

God and **you**
God and **you**
Lord, just **God** and **you**!

God and **you**
God and **you**
He asked me to say just **God** and **you**!

God and **you**
God and **you**
That's what this is about, **God** and **you**!

God and **you**
God and **you**
Yes, just **God** and **you**!

I Corinthians 1:9
Ephesians 1:3-14

Gail P. Miller

True Love Opened My Heart!
(Song of Gail)

True Love opened my heart and began to sing.
I had no clue what **God** had written within.

His song was sung by
The melodies of **His** own heart.

They only can be heard by an obedient,
humbled and surrendered heart.

True Love opened my heart and began to sing!

I Corinthians 14:15
Ephesians 5:19
James 5:13

True Love Has a Passion for You!

The God of Power!
(Song of Gail)

There is a **God** with **power**
and **He's** the one I serve.

There is a **God** with **power**
and **He's** the one I serve.

There is a **God** with **power**
and **He's** the one I serve.

**His Name is…
El Shaddai, The Almighty God!**

Genesis 17:1
Genesis 35:11
Psalm 91:1
Revelation 11:17

Gail P. Miller

Here Am I Lord!
(Song of Gail)

Here am I.
Here am I, **Lord.**
Here am I knocking at **Your** gate.

Here am I.
Here am I, **Lord.**
Here am I waiting in my place.

Here am I.
Here am I, **Lord.**
Here am I seeking for **Your** face.

Here am I.
Here am I, **Lord.**
Here am I anticipating our date.

Here am I.
Here am I, **Lord.**
Here am I calling for my sake.

Here am I.
Here am I, **Lord.**
Here am I listening for **Your** voice.

Here am I.
Here am I, **Lord.**
Here am I and I have made **You** my choice.

Joshua 24:15
Psalm 37:25
Hebrews 13:5-6

True Love Has a Passion for You!

What Can I Do?
(Song of Gail)

What can I do to comfort **You**?
What can I do to comfort **You, Lord**?
What can I do to comfort **You, Lord,**
over the lose of **Your** loved ones?

Tell me, what can I do?

"Sing to **Me** out of **your** heart!"

Romans 8:26-27
Ephesians 5:19
Colossians 3:15-16

Gail P. Miller

Blow On Your Garden!
(Song of Gail)

Blow on **Your** garden, **Lord,**
So that **You** can smell of **its** fragrance.

Blow on **Your** garden, **Lord,**
So that **You** can taste of **its** seasoned spices.

Blow on **Your** garden, **Lord,**
So that **You** can eat of **Your** favorite fruits.

Blow on **Your** garden, **Lord,**
So that **You** can come and help **Yourself**!

Blow on **Your** garden, **Lord,**
So that **You** can make **Your** presence known.

Blow on **Your** garden, **Lord,**
So that **You** can bring **Your** friends.

Blow on **Your** garden, **Lord,**
So that **You** can have **Your** fill.

Breathe on **me**... **Lord!**

Genesis 2:8; 3:8
Song of Solomon 4:12, 16
Isaiah 58:11

True Love Has a Passion for You!

My Heart
(Song of Gail)

My heart I bring to **You,** my **Master!**

My heart I bring to **You,** my **Lord!**

My heart I bring to **You,** my **King!**

My heart I bring to **You,** my **Father!**

My heart I bring to **You,** my **Friend!**

My heart I bring to **You,** my **Husband!**

You requested my heart and my heart I will bring.

My **Lord**, My **Father**, My **King!**

Matthew 5:8
Matthew 6:21
Colossians 3:12-16

Gail P. Miller

He Took Me!
(Song of Gail)

He took **me** to a place where
There were no boundaries:
No limits
No stops
No sides
No bottoms
No tops

He took **me** to a place where
Nothing could be measured:
No height
No width
No length
No depth

He carried **me** to a place where
There was no time:
No seconds
No minutes
No hours
No months or days
No years or seasons

He lifted **me** to this place that
Wasn't like anything I had ever seen:

True Love Has a Passion for You!

Nothing I had experienced
Nothing I had touched
Nothing I had smelled
Nothing I had tasted
Nothing I could say
Nothing at all.

I turned to **Him** and asked,
"What is this place?"

He lovingly smiled and said,
"This place is **Me!**"

Acts 17:28
John 17:20-26
Ephesians 1:3

Gail P. Miller

Words of Wisdom

Words of Knowledge

Words of Exhortation

True Love Has a Passion for You!

Denominationalism

Long flowing clothes make sure **you** cover **your** toes.
Elbows and knees, how long are **your** sleeves?

"For the Lord does not *see* as man sees; for man
looks at the outward appearance, but the
Lord looks at the heart."

D e n o m i n a t i o n a l i smmmmmm
come from behind **your** wall!

We believe like this, but **you** believe like that.
We speak like this, but **you** speak like that.
We baptize like this, but **you** baptize like that. We
worship like this, but **you** worship like that.

"There is one body and one Spirit, just as
you were called in one hope of your calling."

D e n o m i n a t i o n a l i smmmmmm
come from behind **your** wall!

You can't go here and **you** can't go there.
You can't do this and **you** can't do that.
"Who also made us sufficient as ministers

of the new covenant?
Not of the letter,
but of the Spirit; for the letter kills,
but the Spirit gives life."

D e n o m i n a t i o n a l i smmmmmm
come from behind **your** wall!

You compare **yourselves** with **yourselves** and think highly of **yourselves** because **you** are trying to make a name for **yourselves**.

"For we dare not class ourselves or compare ourselves with those who commend themselves. But they, measuring themselves by themselves, and comparing themselves among themselves, are not wise."

"God resists the proud,
But gives grace to the humble."

D e n o m i n a t i o n a l i smmmmmm
come from behind **your** wall!

I am of Paul. I am of Apollos. I am of Luther. I am of Calvin. I am of Wesley and I am of so and so.

"Is Christ divided?"

D e n o m i n a t i o n a l i smmmmmm
come from behind **your** wall!

Lutheran, Protestant, Methodist, Evangelicals, Holiness, Pentecostal. Baptist, Foursquare Gospel, Assemblies of God, Church of God in Christ, and so on.
Is **Jim Crow** in the **Church?**

"That there should be no schism in the body, but *that* the members should have the same care for one another."

D e n o m i n a t i o n a l i smmmmmm
come from behind **your** wall!

Doctrines of men, dogmas, creeds, traditions, legalism, myths, fables, or old wise tales; aren't they all proclamations of self emancipations?

"Inasmuch as these people draw near
with their mouths
And honor me with their lips,
But their heart is far
from Me,
And their fear toward Me is taught by
The commandment of men."

Gail P. Miller

Denominationalismmmmmm
come from behind **your** wall!

Even the First Amendment states, "Congress shall make no law respecting of an establishment of religion."

"For the sons of this world are more shrewd in their generation than the sons of light."

Denominationalismmmmmm
come from behind **your** wall!

The Berlin Wall, the Great Wall of China and the **Denominational Wall**, aren't they all man made?

"Now I plead with you, brethren, by the name of our Lord Jesus Christ, that you all speak the same thing, and *that* there be no divisions among you, but *that* you be perfectly joined together in the same mind and in the same judgment."

Denominationalismmmmmm
come from behind **your** wall!

Denominationalism is segregation _**Personified!**_

"But Jesus knew their thoughts, and said to them: "Every kingdom divided against itself is brought to desolation, and every city or house divided against itself will not stand."

A divided church… cannot STAND!

I Samuel 16:7
Ephesians 4:4
II Corinthians 3:6
II Corinthians 10:12
James 4:6b
I Corinthians 1:13
I Corinthians 12:25
Isaiah 29:13
Luke 16:8b
I Corinthians 1:10
Matthew 12:23

Gail P. Miller

But God Said!
(Words of Exhortation)

You don't know what he did to me.
You don't know how she treated me.
You don't know how it felt.

<u>**But God said**</u>, "And whenever you stand praying, if you have anything against anyone,
    forgive him, that your Father in heaven may
        also
    forgive you your trespasses. But if you do not forgive, neither will your Father in heaven forgive your trespasses."
    —Matthew 6:14-15; Mark 11:25-26

You don't know what happened to me.
You don't know why they did what they did to me.
You don't know how the memories affect me.
You don't know how **I** feel.

<u>**But God said**</u>, "Honor your father and your mother,
    that your days may be long upon
    the land which the Lord your God
    is giving you."
    —Exodus 20:12; Ephesians 6:1-3

True Love Has a Passion for You!

You don't know that he wasn't there for me.
You don't know that she wasn't there for me.
You don't know the guilt or the shame I carry.
You don't know what they put me through.
You just don't know!

But God said, "So My heavenly Father also will do to you if each of you from your heart does not forgive his brother his trespasses."
—Matthew 6:14-15; 18:35

You don't know what I had to do.
You don't know what I had to say.
You don't know what I had to cover up.
You have no idea!

But God said, "For if you forgive men their trespasses, your heavenly Father will also forgive you. But if you do not forgive men their trespasses, neither will your Father forgive your trespasses."
—Matthew 6: 14-15; Luke 17: 3-4

But that's not fair. **I** am the one who was hurt and **somebody** has to pay!

WHAT DID GOD SAY?

Gail P. Miller

Forgive
(Words of Exhortation)

When **you** don't forgive,
"Neither will the **Father** forgive **you!**"

When **you** don't forgive from **your** heart,
"Neither will the **Father** forgive **you!**"

Seventy times seven in a day **you** must forgive, if **your** brother/sister comes **your** way.

When **you** don't forgive,
"Neither will the **Father** forgive **you!**"

When **you** don't forgive from **your** heart,
"Neither will the **Father** forgive **you!**"

Forgive us, **Lord.**

Forgive us, **Lord.**

For we have sinned against **You!**

Matthew 11: 25-26
Matthew 18: 22-35
James 4:17

True Love Has a Passion for You!

His Song!
(Word of Knowledge)

He won't reveal **His Song**
because **you** are the number one singer.

He won't reveal **His Song**
because **you** are at the top of the charts.

He won't reveal **His Song**
because **you** have won some music awards.

He won't reveal **His song**
because **you** have walked many a red carpet.

He won't reveal **His song**
because **you** are Bishop, Elder, Reverend, preacher, teacher, evangelist, brother, sister or Doctor so and so.

He will only reveal **His Song**
to **you** whom **He** can trust because **God** and **His Angelic Hosts** are going to sing along.

Exodus 15:1-21
I Chronicles 6:31
II Chronicles 5:12-14
II Chronicles 20:20-22
Psalm 40:3
Zephaniah 3:17
John 4:23-24
Revelation 5:9
Revelation 15:3

Gail P. Miller

His Voice!
(Words of Wisdom and Exhortation)

There are many voices in the land
So, tune **your** ear to hear **His Voice**.

His Voice is full of soothing, healing and delivering oil.
So, tune **your** ear to hear **His Voice.**

His Voice can stop a raging, stormy wind.
So, tune **your** ear to hear **His** still small voice.

His Voice only, has the power to bring forth **His** purpose for **your** life on the earth.

"**My** sheep know **My Voice!**"
So, listen for **His Voice**!

Proverbs 19:21
John 10:3-4
Hebrews 3:7-19

True Love Has a Passion for You!

He's Calling You!
(Words of Knowledge and Exhortation)

He's calling **you**. Can't **you** hear **Him**?
    He's calling **you** not to blame.

He's calling **you**. Can't **you** hear **Him**?
    He's calling just the same.

He's calling **you**. Can't **you** hear **Him**?
    He's calling to reveal **His** fame.

He's calling **you**. Can't **you** hear **Him**?
    He's calling and it's **your** sin that is **His** aim.

He's calling **you**. Can't **you** hear **Him**?
    He's calling and it's **your** heart **He** wants to tame.

Let *those* who have an ear, hear
Him <u>summoning</u> **you** by name!

I Corinthians 2:9
Hebrews 3:7-19
Revelation 2:7, 11, 17, 29

Gail P. Miller

He's Calling for Holy People!
(Words of Wisdom)

He's calling for a Holy People!
   He's calling for a Holy People!

He's calling for a Holy People!
   He's calling for a Holy People!

He's calling for a Holy People!
   He's calling for a Holy People!

He's calling for a Holy People!
   He's calling for a Holy People!

He's calling for a Holy People!
   He's calling for a Holy People!

He's calling for a Holy People!
   He's calling for a Holy People!

Leviticus 11:44-45
Ephesians 2:19-22
I Peter 1:16

You Don't Know!
(Words of Exhortation)

You don't know
>> when it's going to be **your**
>>>> last call.

He has called **you** over and over again.

You don't know
>> when it's going to be **your**
>>>> last call.

He's called **you** this way and **He's** called **you** that way.

You don't know
>> when it's going to be **your**
>>>> last call.

His mercies are new every day but, when they are over for **you**, **you** will pay!

You don't know
>> when it's going to be **your**
>>>> last call.

He sent **His** servants, **your** neighbors, family members, strangers and even **your** friend, over and over and over again.

You don't know
                when it's going to be **your**
                              <u>last call.</u>

It's not the last call for fame, fortune or alcohol.

_____,
                <u>tonight</u> might be the night **your**
                    soul is required
                    of **YOU!**

                                        Matthew 16:26
                                          Luke 12:20
                                      James 4:13-17

True Love Has a Passion for You!

Is Your Name Written?
(Words of Wisdom and Exhortation)

Is **your** name written in the
    Lamb's Book of Life
        Or
was it entered and then blotted out?

Is **your** name written in the
    Lamb's Book of Life
        Or
are **you** not willing to give up **your** life?

Is **your** name written in the
    Lamb's Book of Life
        Or
are **you** in darkness and without sight?

Is **your** name written in the
    Lamb's Book of Life
        Or
do **you** plan on putting up a fight?

Is **your** name written in the
    Lamb's Book of Life
        Or
do **your** beliefs have **you** wrapped up tight?

Gail P. Miller

Is **your** name written
Or
did **you** even know there was… such a **Book**?

Exodus 32:32-33
Matthew 16:24-25
Revelation 13:8

True Love Has a Passion for You!

What Excuse Will You Give?
(Words of Knowledge)

The sun preaches.
The moon preaches.
The stars preach.
The heavens preach.
The winds preach.
The snow preaches.
The rain preaches.
The rainbow preaches.
The flowers preach.
The birds preach.
The plants preach.
The trees preach.
The waters preach.
The earth preaches.

All that **God** has created lifts up their voices day in and day out in their season.

What excuse will you give… for not <u>believing</u>?

Psalm 19:1-6
Psalm 75:1
Psalm 97:6
Isaiah 55:12

Gail P. Miller

If God Be for You!
(Words of Exhortation)

If **God** be for **you**,
"No weapon formed against you shall prosper."
—Isaiah 54:17a

If **God** be for **you**,
"You are of God, little children, and have
overcome them, because He who is in you
is greater than he who is in the world."
—I John 4:4

If **God** be for **you**,
"Behold, I give you the authority to
trample on serpents and scorpions, and
over all the power of the enemy, and nothing shall by
any means hurt you."
—Luke 10:19

If **God** be for **you**,
"You did not choose Me, but I chose
you and appointed you that you should go
and bear fruit, and that your fruit should
remain, that whatever you ask the Father
in My name he may give you."
—John 15:16

True Love Has a Passion for You!

If **God** be for **you**,
"And these signs will follow those who believe: In My name they will cast out demons; they will speak with new tongues; they will take up serpents; and if they drink anything deadly, it will by no means hurt them; they will lay hands on the sick, and they will recover."
—Mark 16:17-18

If **God** be for **you**,
"Yet in all these thing we are **more than conquerors** through Him who loved us."
—Romans 8:37

If **God** be for **you**,
"*Let your* conduct **be** without covetousness; *be* content with such things as you have. For He Himself has said, I will never leave you nor forsake you."
—Hebrews 13:5

If **God** be for **you**,
"What then shall we say to these things? If God *is* for us, who *can be* against us?"
—Romans 8:31

Is…**God** for **you**?

Gail P. Miller

You Are Nothing Without Him!
(Words of Wisdom and Knowledge)

You are only
a vessel that pours **God's** drink.

You are only
the bowl that contains **God's** meat.

You are only
an instrument that carries **God's** message.

You are only
a clay pot that receives **God's** power.

You are only
a sheep that does **God's** will.

You are only
dust that is known as **God's** ground.

You are only
the candle that shines **God's** light.

One plants, one waters
but
without **Him**… <u>nothing</u>!

Genesis 2:7
Proverbs 20:27
I Corinthians 3:7

True Love Has a Passion for You!

You Are!
(Word of Knowledge)

You are…the "just."
You are…a "holy nation."
You are…the "redeemed."
You are…the "restored."
You are…the "saints."
You are…the "gifted."
You are…the "blessed."
You are…the "beloved."
You are…the "forgiven."
You are…the "reconciled."
You are…the "called out."
You are…a "living stone."
You are…a "royal priesthood."
You are…the "bride of **Christ**."
You are…the "temple of **God**."
You are…the "apple of **His** eye."
You are…a "chosen generation."
You are…the "heirs of salvation."
You are…the "liberated in **Christ**."
You are…the "ambassador of **Christ**."
You are…the "church of the **Living God**."
You are…made in the "image and likeness of **God**."
You are…the "righteousness of **God** in **Christ Jesus**."
You are…the "sons and daughters of the **Lord Almighty**."

Jesus is…**your** identity!

Romans 1:17	Ephesians 1:6-7	Hebrews 1:14
I Peter 2:9	Romans 5:8-10	Luke 4:18
Psalm 107:2	I Peter 2:5	Romans 5:20-21
Psalm 23:3	Revelations 21:9	I Timothy 3:15
Revelations 8:3-4	I Corinthians 3:17	Genesis 1:26-28
Ephesians 4:7-8	Zechariah 2:8	II Corinthians 3:17

Gail P. Miller

You Are His Bride!
(Words of Wisdom and Exhortation)

"But the wiser took oil in their vessels
with their lamps."
—Matthew 25:4

He promised **Him** a bride without spot or wrinkle.

"Beware of the leaven of the Pharisees,
which is hypocrisy.
"For there is nothing covered that will
not be revealed, nor hidden that will not be
known.
Therefore what ever you have spoken in
the dark will be heard in the light,
and what you have spoken in the ear in inner
rooms will be proclaimed on the housetops."
—Luke 12:1-3

He promised **Him** a bride without spot or wrinkle.

'The stone which the builders rejected
Has become the chief cornerstone'?
"Whoever falls on that stone will be

broken; but on whomever it falls, it will grind him to powder."
—Luke 20:17-18

He promised **Him** a bride without spot or wrinkle.

"Every branch in Me that does not bear fruit He takes away; and every branch that bears fruit He prunes, that it may bear more fruit."
—John 15:2

He promised **Him** a bride without spot or wrinkle.

"Therefore, having these promises, beloved, let us cleanse ourselves from all filthiness of the flesh and spirit, perfecting holiness in the fear of God."
—II Corinthians 7:1

He promised **Him** a bride without spot or wrinkle.

"For godly sorrow produces repentance *leading* to salvation, not to be regretted; but the sorrow of the world produces death."
—II Corinthians 7:10

He promised **Him** a bride without spot or wrinkle.

"Work out your own salvation with fear and trembling;
for it is God who works in you both to will and to do for His good pleasure."
—Philippians 2:12b-13

He promised **Him** a bride without spot or wrinkle.

"For God has not given us a spirit of fear, but of power and of love and of a sound mind."
—II Timothy 1:7

He promised **Him** a bride without spot or wrinkle.

"My son, do not despise the chastening of the LORD,
Nor be discouraged when you are rebuked by Him;
For whom the LORD loves He chastens,
And scourges every son whom He receives."
—Hebrews 12:5-6

He promised **Him** a bride without spot or wrinkle.

True Love Has a Passion for You!

"Behold, I am coming as a thief.
Blessed is he who watches, and keeps his
garments, lest he walk naked and they see
his shame."
—Revelation 16:15

He promised **Him** a bride without spot or wrinkle.

"that He might sanctify and cleanse her
with the washing of water by the word,
that He might present her to Himself a
glorious church, not having spot, or wrinkle,
or any such thing, but that she should be
holy and without
blemish."
—Ephesians 5:26-27

If **you** have accepted **Christ** as **your** personal Savior,
then **you** are **His** bride.
Let **Him** prepare <u>**you**</u>!

Gail P. Miller

He Has a Right!
(Words Wisdom and Exhortation)

He has a right to **your** heart.

He has a right to **your** soul.

He has a right to **your** body.

He has a right to **your** mind.

He has a right to **your** strength.

He has a right to **your** life.

He paid the price so,

He has the right!

Deuteronomy 6:4-5
Mark 12:29-31
I Corinthians 6:20

True Love Has a Passion for You!

Are You Sleeping with Your Sister?
(Words of Knowledge and Exhortation)

But I'm a man, it's my nature.
Are **you** sleeping with **your** sister?
But I have needs.
Are **you** sleeping with **your** sister?
But we're engaged.
Are **you** sleeping with **your** sister?
But we love each other.
Are **you** sleeping with **your** sister?
But we're good friends.
Are **you** sleeping with **your** sister?
But everybody is doing it.
Are **you** sleeping with **your** sister?
But what **you** don't know won't hurt **you.**
Are **you** sleeping with **your** sister?
But my wife doesn't understand me like she does.
Are **you** sleeping with **your** sister?
But she…
Are **you** sleeping with **your** sister?
But…

She's **your** sister!

Exodus 20:14
I Corinthians 6:19
Ephesians 5:3

Gail P. Miller

Your Sin!
(Words of Knowledge)

It was **your** sin that…
caused **Him** to come.

It was **your** sin that…
caused **Him** to draw near **you**.

It was **your** sin that…
caused **Him** to reveal **Himself** to **you**.

It was **your** sin that…
caused **Him** pain.

It was **your** sin that…
caused **Him** to be afflicted.

It was **your** sin that…
caused **Him** to shed **His** blood.

It was **your** sin that…
caused **Him** to be put to death.

It was **your** sin that…
caused **you** to die spiritually.

True Love Has a Passion for You!

It was **your** sin that…
caused **you** separation.

It was **your** sin that…
caused **you** not be able to touch **Him.**

It was **your** sin that…
caused **you** to worship **Him** from afar.

Your sin
keeps…
you from **Him**!

Isaiah 53:5
Romans 3:23
Ephesians 2:13
Hebrews 9:24-28

Gail P. Miller

Separated from Him
(Prophetic Words of Knowledge and Exhortation)

Never again will **you** *be able to* feel the wind of **His Spirit**.

Never again will **you** *be able to* sense **His** manifested presence.

Never again will **you** *be able to* sit with **Him**.

Never again will **you** *be able to* walk with **Him**.

Never again will **you** *be able to* feel **His** breadth on **your** face.

Never again will **you** *be able to* smell **His Aroma**.

Never again will **you** *be able to* taste of **His Goodness**.

Never again will **you** *be able to* have intimacy with **Him**.

Never again will **you** *be able to* know **His Ways**.

Never again will **you** *be able to* be filled with **His Glory**.

Never again will **you** *be able to* know **His Mercy**.

Never again will **you** *be able to* have **His Favor**.

Never again will **you** *be able to* hear **His Voice**.

Never again will **you** *be able to* learn of **His Truth**.

Never again will **you** *be able to* carry **His Righteousness**.

True Love Has a Passion for You!

Never again will **you** *be able to* worship **Him**.

Never again will **you** *be able to* lift **you**r voice in praise to **Him**.

Never again will **you** *be able to* possess **His** peace.

Never again will **you** *be able to* receive **His** blessings and rewards.

Never again will **you** *be able to* commune with **Him**.

Never again will **you** *be able to* eat from the **Tree of Life**.

Never again will **you** *be able to* fellowship with **Him** in paradise.

I will declare to them, "**I** never knew **you**."

Never, ever, ever again!

Matthew 7:21-23
John 8:21

Gail P. Miller

You Can Give!
(Words of Knowledge and Exhortation)

You can give
Him your pain.

You can give
Him your hurt.

You can give
Him your situation.

You can give
Him your family.

You can give
Him your relationships.

You can give
Him your things.

You can give
Him your ministry.

You can give
Him your praise.

True Love Has a Passion for You!

You can give
Him your worship.

You can give
Him your tithe.

You can give
Him your offering.

You can give
Him your body.

But if **you**
do not give
Him your <u>heart,</u>
then **He** doesn't
have **<u>You!</u>**

Deuteronomy 8:2
I Samuel 16:7
Isaiah 29:13
Hosea 10:2
Matthew 6:19-21, 24

Gail P. Miller

Are You Keeping Him from What He Deserves?
(Words of Knowledge and Exhortation)

He laid down **His** life!
Are **you** keeping **Him** from getting what **He** deserves?

He shed **His** blood!
Are **you** keeping **Him** from getting what **He** deserves?

He was tempted in all points just as we are!
Are **you** keeping **Him** from getting what **He** deserves?

He paid the ultimate price!
Are **you** keeping **Him** from getting what **He** deserves?

He died on the cross!
Are **you** keeping **Him** from getting what **He** deserves?

He went into hell and now has the keys of
death and hell!
Are **you** keeping **Him** from getting what **He** deserves?

He is the resurrection!
Are **you** keeping **Him** from getting what **He** deserves?

He sits at the right hand of **God** in power!
Are **you** keeping **Him** from getting what **He** deserves?

He deserves **You!**

John 3:16
Ephesians 1:3-8
Ephesians 2:8-10
Revelation 1:18

True Love Has a Passion for You!

Give Him What He Asks For!
(Words of Wisdom and Exhortation)

Your heart, give it to **Him.**
Your soul, give it to **Him.**
Your mind, give it to **Him.**
Your body, give it to **Him.**
Your strength, give it to **Him.**
Your ways, give them to **Him.**
Your plans, give them to **Him.**
Your dreams, give them to **Him.**
Your desires, give them to **Him.**
Your possessions, give them to **Him.**
Your relationships, give them to **Him.**
Your trust, give it to **Him.**
Your life, give it to **Him.**
Why… **He** <u>needs</u> **You!**

Deuteronomy 10:12; 30:6
Matthew 16:25-27
Mark 12:29-30
Luke 9:23-24

Gail P. Miller

The King's Table!
(Words of Knowledge)

Who sits at the King's table?

Those who have been…invited!

Psalm 23:5
II Samuel 9:7-13
Luke 14:8-11
Luke 14:16-24
Revelation 19:6-9

True Love Has a Passion for You!

The Presence of God
(Words of Wisdom)

In the presence of ***God is*** safety.
In the presence of ***God is*** prosperity.
In the presence of ***God is*** health.
In the presence of ***God is*** deliverance.
In the presence of ***God is*** wealth.
In the presence of ***God is*** understanding.
In the presence of ***God is*** knowledge.
In the presence of ***God is*** wisdom.
In the presence of ***God is*** peace.
In the presence of ***God is*** love.
In the presence of ***God is*** joy.
In the presence of ***God is*** liberty.
In the presence of ***God is*** a gift.

The presence of ***God is*** everything!

Psalm 16:11
Acts 2:28
II Corinthians 3:17

Gail P. Miller

Fellowship
(Words of Wisdom)

He will create in **you** a desire to be near **Him.**

He will create in **you** a desire to know **Him.**

He will create in **you** a desire to touch **Him.**

He will create in **you** a desire to seek **Him.**

He will create in **you** a desire to walk with **Him.**

He will create in **you** a desire to talk with **Him.**

He will create in **you** a desire to hear **Him.**

He will create in **you** a desire to love **Him.**

He will create in **you** a desire to be with **Him.**

But only…

if **you** pursue the call to fellowship with **Him**!

Psalm 37:4
I Corinthians 1:9
Philippians 3:8-10

True Love Has a Passion for You!

His Blood
(Words of Wisdom)

He purchased **you** with
> **His Blood.**

He delivered **you** with
> **His Blood.**

He healed **you** with
> **His Blood.**

He saved **you** with
> **His Blood.**

He cleansed **you** with
> **His Blood.**

He redeemed **you** with
> **His Blood.**

The price was…
> **His Blood.**

Leviticus 17:11
Hebrews 9:22
Matthew 26: 27-28
Acts 20:28

Gail P. Miller

The Blood Speaks!
(Prophetic Words of Wisdom)

Mercy, Mercy, Mercy,

Mercy, Mercy, Mercy,

Mercy, Mercy, Mercy,

Mercy, Mercy, Mercy,

Mercy, Mercy, Mercy,

Mercy, Mercy, Mercy,

Mercy, Mercy, Mercy!

Mercy, Mercy, Mercy!

Cries the Blood!

Genesis 4:10
Leviticus 17:11
Hebrews 12:24

True Love Has a Passion for You!

Grace
(Words of Wisdom and Exhortation)

You can't praise it up.

You can't sing it up.

You can't preach it up.

You can't tongue it up.

You can't prophesy it up.

You can't pray it up.

You can't buy it up.

You can't work it up.

You can't charge it up.

You can't lay it up.

You can't take it up.

You can't bring it up.

Grace...is a free gift!

John 1:17
Ephesians 2:8

Gail P. Miller

God the Butcher
(Words of Wisdom and Knowledge)

God chopped **Jesus** up for **you**
and gave **Him** as a Heave Offering.

God chopped **Jesus** up for **you**
and gave **Him** as a Wave Offering.

God chopped **Jesus** up for **you**
and gave **Him** as a Peace Offering.

God chopped **Jesus** up for **you**
and gave **Him** as a Sin Offering.

God chopped **Jesus** up for **you**
and gave **Him** as a Burnt Offering.

God chopped **Jesus** up for **you**
and gave **Him** as a Grain Offering.

God chopped **Jesus** up for **you**
and gave **Him** as a Trespass Offering.

God pierced **Jesus** in **His** side for **you**
and poured out **His** blood for a Libation Offering.

True Love Has a Passion for You!

God Himself ate of His fat

So… come, eat and drink for **God,** has made **Jesus** accessible to **you!**

Leviticus 1:3; 2:1; 3:1; 4:3; 5:6; 7:14, 30; 23:13
John 3:16
I Corinthians 11:24-25
Hebrews 10:5-10

Gail P. Miller

The Carcass
(Words of Wisdom)

Out of **His** carcass comes **your** supply.

Out of **His** carcass comes **your** meat.

Out of **His** carcass comes **your** drink.

Out of **His** carcass comes **your** bread.

Out of **His** carcass comes **your** meal.

Out of **His** carcass comes **your** light.

Out of **His** carcass comes **your** nourishment.

His living carcass is **your** <u>lifeline</u>!

Matthew 24:28
Luke 17:37
John 6:35
John 6:53-58

True Love Has a Passion for You!

In Him!
(Words of Wisdom and Knowledge)

In **Him**, **you** have life.
In **Him**, **you** have joy.
In **Him**, **you** have peace.
In **Him**, **you** have safety.
In **Him**, **you** have love.
In **Him**, **you** have health.
In **Him**, **you** have correction.
In **Him**, **you** have discipline.
In **Him**, **you** have salvation.
In **Him**, **you** have understanding.
In **Him**, **you** have vision.
In **Him**, **you** have wisdom.
In **Him**, **you** have knowledge.
In **Him**, **you** have spiritual gifts.
In **Him**, **you** have relationship.
In **Him**, **you** have fellowship.
In **Him**, **you** have intimacy.
In **Him**, **you** have pleasure.
In **Him**, **you** have purpose.
In **Him**, **you** have.
In **Him**, **you**
In **Him**,
Him

Acts 17:28
Colossians 1:16-21

Gail P. Miller

Who Is Jesus?
(Words of Wisdom and Knowledge)

Who is **Jesus?**
The First Fruits.

Who is **Jesus**?
The Bread of Life.

Who is **Jesus**?
The Tithe.

Who is **Jesus**?
The Passover Meal!

Who is **Jesus**?
The Holy Spirit.

Who is **Jesus**?
The Word.

Who is **Jesus**?
The Garment of Praise.

Who is **Jesus**?
The Armor of God.

True Love Has a Passion for You!

Who is **Jesus**?
Language.

Who is **Jesus**?
The Door.

Who is **Jesus**?
The Voice of God.

Who is **Jesus**?
Your Elder Brother.

Who is **Jesus**?
The Lamb.

Who is **Jesus**?
The Set Price.

Who is **Jesus**?
Prayer.

Who is **Jesus**?
The Resurrection.

Who is **Jesus**?
The Expressed Image of God.

Gail P. Miller

Who is **Jesus**?
True Love.

Who is **Jesus**?
The Circumcision.

Who is **Jesus**?
The Cleft.

Who is **Jesus**?
Intercession.

Who is **Jesus**?
The Completed Work.

Who is **Jesus**?
Eternity.

Who is **Jesus**?
Rest.

Who is **Jesus?**
Rescue.

Who is **Jesus**?
The Light of Men.

True Love Has a Passion for You!

Who is **Jesus?**
The Father.

Who is **Jesus?**
The Foundation.

Who is **Jesus**?
The Bridegroom.

Who is **Jesus**?
Wisdom.

Who is **Jesus**?
Knowledge.

Who is **Jesus**?
Understanding.

Who is **Jesus**?
Peace.

Who is **Jesus?**
The Cup of God.

Who is **Jesus?**
Judgment.

Gail P. Miller

Who is **Jesus?**
Truth.

Who is **Jesus?**
Time.

Who is **Jesus?**
Jesus was.

Who is **Jesus?**
Jesus shall be.

Who is **Jesus?**
Everything!

Jesus is!

Exodus 3:14
Exodus 33:22
John 14:6
I Corinthians 11: 24-25
Colossians 1:16-17

True Love Has a Passion for You!

He Is
(Words of Wisdom and Knowledge)

He is **your** *healing.*
He is **your** *comfort.*
He is **your** *deliverance.*
He is **your** *glory.*
He is **your** *love.*
He is **your** *resurrection.*
He is **your** *faith.*
He is **your** *bread.*
He is **your** *meat.*
He is **your** *protection.*
He is **your** *supply.*
He is **your** *truth.*
He is **your** *power.*
He is **your** *destination.*
He is **your** *transportation.*
He is **your** *covering.*
He is **your** *relationship.*
He is **your** *salvation.*
He is **your** *peace.*
He is **your** *joy.*
He is **your** *gift.*
He is **your** *grace.*
He is **your** *liberty.*
He is *it.*
He is *why.*

He is **y*ours*!**

Exodus 3:14
Exodus 33:22
Colossians 1:16-20
Revelation 1:8

Gail P. Miller

He was Slain
(Words of Wisdom and Knowledge)

He was slain from the foundation of the world

He was slain
He was slain

He was slain from the foundation of the world

He was slain
He was slain

The world and all creation
lay on the foundation
of **His** slaughter

I Corinthians 3:11
Colossians 1:16-17
Revelation 13:8

True Love Has a Passion for You!

Silently!
(Words of Wisdom and Exhortation)

For **you**,
The **Lamb** gave up
His blood!

For **you**,
The **Lamb** gave up
His inner parts!

For **you**,
The **Lamb** gave up
His fat!

For **you**,
The **Lamb** gave up
His body!

For **you**,
The **Lamb** gave up
His life!

For **you**,
The **Lamb** gave up
His soul!

But
He did it all,
Silently!

Isaiah 53:7-12
Acts 8:32-33

Gail P. Miller

He's Coming Soon!
(Words of Exhortation)

He's coming soon.
Have **you** accepted **Him**?

He's coming soon.
Will **you** go back with **Him**?

He's coming soon.
What are **you** waiting for?

He's coming soon.
But why is **He** delayed?

He's coming soon.
He doesn't want to leave without **you.**

He is… soon to come!

Matthew 24:3-44
Mark 13:5-37
Revelation 22:7, 12-13, 20

True Love Has a Passion for You!

The Choice
(Words of Knowledge and Exhortation)

He *chose* **you**

and gave **you** the *choice*

to *choose* **Him** back.

So… it's the *choice* **you** make

that makes the difference.

Deuteronomy 30:14
Proverbs 18:21
John 3:16
Romans 10:9-13

Gail P. Miller

The Seed!
(Word of Knowledge)

"And I will put enmity
Between you and the woman
And between your seed and her Seed."
—Genesis 3:15a

Seed!

"And as he sowed, some seed fell by the
wayside; and the birds came and devoured them."
—Matthew 13:4

Seed!

"Some fell on stony places where they
did not have much earth; and they immediately
sprang up because they had no depth of earth.
But when the sun was up they were
scorched, and because they had no root
they withered away."
—Matthew 13:5-6

Seed!

"And some fell among thorns, and the
thorns sprang up and choked them."
—Matthew 13:7

Seed!
"But others fell on good ground and
yielded a crop: some a hundred fold, some

True Love Has a Passion for You!

sixty, some thirty."
—Matthew 13:8

Seed!

"Having been born again, not of corruptible seed but incorruptible, through the word of God which lives and abides for ever,"
—I Peter 1:23

The Seed became flesh!
—John 1:14

Gail P. Miller

The Blessing!
(Word of Knowledge)

"And in you all the families of the earth shall be blessed."
—Genesis 12:3b

What is the Blessing?

"If I will not open for you the
windows of heaven
And pour out for you *such* blessings
That *there will* not *be* **room enough** to
receive it."
—Malachi 3:10

What is the Blessing?

"Blessed *be* the God and Father of our
Lord Jesus Christ, who has bless us with
every spiritual blessing in the heavenly
places in Christ."
—Ephesians 1:3

What is the Blessing?

"that the blessing of Abraham might
come upon the Gentiles in Christ Jesus,
that we might receive the promise of the
Spirit through faith,"
—Galatians 3:14

God and **His Word** are one.
So…who is the **Blessing**?
—I John 5:7

True Love Has a Passion for You!

Change
(Words of Wisdom)

Things change.

People change.

Cultures change.

Ages change.

Seasons change.

Systems change.

Times change.

Lives change.

But God and His Word
Never change!

Malachi 3:6
Hebrews 6:18

Gail P. Miller

It's About Him!
(Words of Exhortation)

Worship;
It's about **Him!**

Praise;
It's about **Him!**

Church;
It's about **Him!**

Singing;
It's about **Him!**

Studying;
It's about **Him!**

Preaching;
It's about **Him!**

Teaching;
It's about **Him!**

Evangelism;
It's about **Him!**

Isn't it all…about **Him?**

Psalm 34: 1-3
John 4:23-24

Press In!
(Words of Exhortation)

Press in
Press in
Press in to **Him**
Press in

Press in
Press in
Don't let **Him** go
until **you** know
Press in to **Him**
Press in

Press in
Press in
Press in to **Him**
Press in

Break through the flesh
as **you** continue to press
Press in to **Him**
Press in

Press in
Press in
Press in to **Him**
Press in

Gail P. Miller

Press in far
so **He** can tell **you** who **you** really are
Press in to **Him**
Press in

Press in
Press in
Press in to **Him**
Press in

He drew **you** near
so **He** could break **your** fear
Press in to **Him**
Press in

Press in
Press in
Press in to **Him**
Press in

Do not stop
until **you** harvest **your** crop
Press in to **Him**
Press in

Press!

Genesis 32:24-28
Matthew 7:7-11
Philippians 3:12-14
Colossians 3:1-4

True Love Has a Passion for You!

Springs of the Heart!
(Words of Wisdom and Exhortation)

God's Life springs from **your** heart.
God's Love springs from **your** heart.
God's Fruit springs from **your** heart.
God's Spirit springs from **your** heart.
God's Gifts spring from **your** heart.

As **His** offspring,
"Keep **your** heart with all diligence,
For out of it *spring* the issues of life."

Proverbs 4:23
John 4:14

Gail P. Miller

Waiting for You!
(Words of Knowledge and Exhortation)

True Love has been waiting
for **you** to come to **His** gate.

True Love has been waiting
for **you** since the beginning of time.

True Love has been waiting
for **you** to call out **His** name.

True Love has been waiting
for **you** to break through the flesh.

True Love has been waiting
for **you** to make the right move.

True Love has been waiting
for **you** to let it all go.

True Love has been waiting
for **you** to come back to **Him.**

True Love has been waiting
for **you** to let **Him** in.

True Love is coming back soon
but,
True Love is waiting for **You**!

I Timothy 1:15-16
II Peter 3:9

True Love Has a Passion for You!

You Have a Right to His Love!
(Words of Knowledge and Exhortation)

Because
    you are
        His child
you have a right to sit at **His** feet.

Because
    you are
        His child
you have a right to touch **Him.**

Because
    you are
        His child
you have a right to come to **Him** when **you** are hurting.

Because
    you are
        His child
you have a right to drink from **His** breast.

Because
    you are
        His child
you have a right to be protected by **Him**.

Gail P. Miller

Because
    you are
        His child
you have a right to spend time with **Him**.

Because
    you are
        His child
you have a right to be corrected by **Him**.

Because
    you are
        His child
you have a right to be trained by **Him**.

Because
    you are
        His child
you have a right to partake of **His Love**!

Because
    you are
        His child
you have rights and privileges that are to innumerable to name.

John 17:1-3
Ephesians 1:1-14
II Peter 1:1-8

True Love Has a Passion for You!

You Have Him Forever!
(Prophetic Words of Wisdom)

The communion **you** have with **Him**,
you will have with **Him**…
Forever.

The love **you** share with **Him**,
you will share with **Him**…
Forever.

The joy **you** express toward **Him**,
you will express toward **Him**…
Forever.

The peace **you** experience with **Him**,
you will experience with **Him**…
Forever.

The fruit **you** receive from **Him**,
you will receive from **Him**…
Forever.

The life **you** live in **Him**,
you will live in **Him**…
Forever.

Gail P. Miller

The praise **you** give to **Him**,
you will give to **Him**…
Forever.

The relationship **you** share with **Him**,
you will share with **Him**…
Forever.

The understanding **you** seek of **Him**,
you will seek of **Him**…
Forever.

The oneness **you** maintain with **Him**
you will maintain with **Him**…
Forever.

He and **you** are…
Forever.

John 3:16
John 15:11
Romans 6:23
Romans 11:33
Ephesians 3:19

True Love Has a Passion for You!

He Chose You!
(Words of Exhortation)

Thank the **Lord.**
Thank the **Lord.**
Thank the **Lord** for **He** chose **you** in **Himself** before the foundation of the world**.**

Thank the **Lord.**
Thank the **Lord.**
Thank the **Lord** for **He** predestined **you** by adoption as **His** son.

Thank the **Lord.**
Thank the **Lord.**
Thank the **Lord** for **He** called **you** to **Himself** according to the good pleasure of **His** will.

Thank the **Lord.**
Thank the **Lord.**
Thank the **Lord** for **He** purposed **you** worthy through the blood of **His** only begotten **Son.**

Thank the **Lord.**
Thank the **Lord.**
Thank the **Lord** for **He** chose **you** to be the bride for **His Son.**

Thank **Him** because **you're** the one **He** has chosen!

John 15:16
I Peter 2:9-10
Revelation 22:17

Gail P. Miller

True Love Knew You When!
(Words of Knowledge)

How can **God** use someone like **you?**

Before the plants grew on the earth,

Before any herb came out of the ground,

Before the rain fell from the sky.

He knew **you**...then!!!

Genesis 1:26-27
Genesis 2:4-5
Psalm 90:1-2

True Love Has a Passion for You!

He Made You!
(Words of Wisdom and Exhortation)

For **His** joy,
He made **you.**

For **His** pleasure,
He made **you.**

For carrying **His** Name,
He made **you.**

For **His Son's** bride,
He made **you.**

For **His** temple to dwell in,
He made **you.**

For bringing forth **His Word,**
He made **you.**

For expressing **His Love,**
He made **you.**

For **His** representative in the earth,
He made **you.**

Gail P. Miller

For subduing the earth,
He made **you.**

For fruitfulness and multiplication,
He made **you.**

He said, "It is good,"

When **He** made <u>**you**</u>!

Genesis 1:26-31
I Corinthians 6:19
II Corinthians 6:16
Ephesians 1:5

True Love Has a Passion for You!

Imagine That!!!
(Words of Knowledge)

He desires **you** to love **Him.**

He desires **you** to spend time with **Him.**

He desires **you** to listen to **Him.**

He desires **you** to please **Him.**

He desires **you** to come see about **Him.**

He desires **you** to touch **Him.**

He desires **you** to know **Him.**

He desires **you** to sit in **His** presence.

Imagine that…

He wants **you!**

John 15:4-11
John 17:3, 26
I Corinthians 1:9
Ephesians 1:1-14

Gail P. Miller

Boundaries
(Words of Knowledge)

His identity for **you**
His location for **you**
His path and journey for **you**
His choice of family for **you**
His framework for **you**
His thoughts for **you**
His ways for **you**
His uniqueness for **you**
His will for **you**
His plan for **you**
His purpose for **you**
His good pleasure for **you**
His pre-established laws for **you**
His gifts for **you**
His call for **you**
His blessings for **you**
His promises to **you**

Long before the world was…
His limits were set for **you**!

Psalm 39:4
Psalm 90:10, 12
Acts 17:25-26

True Love Has a Passion for You!

How Is!
(Words of Wisdom and Knowledge)

How vast is **His** Kingdom?

How far is **His** Dominion?

How great is **His** Power?

How clear is **His** Word?

How bright is **His** Light?

How pure is **His** Spirit?

How deep is **His** Love?

All I can tell **you** is…
it will take **you** an eternity to know!

Isaiah 55:8-9
Romans 11:3
Ephesians 3:17-21

Gail P. Miller

Before!
(Words of Knowledge)

Before **My Laws**

Before **My Plans**

Before **My Name**

Before **My Spirit**

Before **My Throne**

Before **My Statutes**

Before **My Purposes**

Before **My Precepts**

Before **My Power**

Before **Me**…*satan* has no authority!

Job 1:6-12; 2:1-6
Luke 4:8
Luke 10:19
Colossians 1:16-18
Colossians 2:9-10

True Love Has a Passion for You!

True Love Brings!
(Words of Knowledge)

True Love brings life.

True Love brings fruit.

True Love brings gifts.

True Love brings light.

True Love brings supply.

True Love brings healing.

True Love brings salvation.

True Love brings wholeness.

True Love brings deliverance.

True Love brings what **you** need.

True Love brought it all!

John 3:16-17
Ephesians 2:4-10
II Thessalonians 2:16
I John 4:9-10

Gail P. Miller

A Different Realm
(Words of Wisdom, Knowledge and Exhortation)

Your sight is different.

Your hearing is different.

Your mind is different.

Your food is different.

Your drink is different.

Your language is different.

Your heart is different.

Your weapons are different.

Christ in **you** is the difference!

Genesis 1:26
Romans 8:1-2, 9
II Corinthians 5:17
Ephesians 4:20-24

True Love Has a Passion for You!

Things
(Words of Wisdom)

"Therefore, if anyone is in Christ, he is a new creation old things have passed away, behold, all things have become new."

"Brethren, I do not count myself to have apprehended; but one thing I do, forgetting those things which are behind and reaching forward to those things which are ahead."

"And God will wipe away every tear from their eyes; there shall be no more death, nor sorrow, nor crying. There shall be no more pain, for the former things have passed away."

"He who overcomes shall inherit all things and I will be his God and he shall be My son."

II Corinthians 5:17
Philippians 3:13
Revelation 21:4
Revelation 21:7

Gail P. Miller

Living Water!
(Words of Wisdom and Exhortation)

Living water
Living water
Come drink from the fountain of
His Living Water!

You can drink from **His** overflowing cup because of **Jesus'** blood **He** took up.

Living water
Living water
come drink from the fountain of
His Living Water!

You who are thirsty, come drink from **His** fountain without price.

Living water
Living water
come drink from the fountain of
His Living Water!

Come drink from… **Jesus!**

Isaiah 55:1
John 4:10; 7:38
Revelation 7:17

True Love Has a Passion for You!

Birds of a Feather Flock Together!
(Words of Wisdom and Exhortation)

"Who provides food for the raven
when its young ones cry to God,
And wander about for lack of food?"
—Job 38:41

"Even the sparrow has found a home,
And the swallow a nest for herself,
Where she may lay her young."
—Psalm 84:3

"There also shall the hawks be gathered,
everyone with her mate."
—Isaiah 34:15

"Even the stork in the heavens
Knows her appointed times
And the turtle dove, the swift, and the swallow
Observe the time of their coming."
—Jeremiah 8:7

"For wherever the carcass is, there the eagles will be gathered together."
—Matthew 24:28

Gail P. Miller

Fragrance of Christ
(Words of Wisdom and Exhortation)

When **you** set **yourself** in agreement with and act on the purpose of **God**,

When **you** set **yourself** in agreement with and act on the plan of **God**,

When **you** set **yourself** in agreement with and act on the instructions of **God**,

When **you** set **yourself** in agreement with and act on the will of **God**,

When **you** set **yourself** in agreement with and act on the call of **God** on **your** life,

Then, "To the one we are the aroma of death leading to death, and to the other we are the aroma of life leading to life."

Are you giving off life and death or just flesh?

What does **God** smell from **you**?

II Corinthians 2:16
John 9:39
I Peter 2:7-9

True Love Has a Passion for You!

That Day!
(Words of Knowledge and Exhortation)

You were <u>Liberated in **Christ**</u> from making a lottery bet, looking for a way out of debt which gives **you** a false hope of having **your** needs met.

When…
in *that Day.*

You were <u>Liberated in **Christ**</u> from drugs a temporary fix for a spiritual bug.

When…
in *that Day.*

You were <u>Liberated in **Christ**</u> from alcohol drowning your pain and sorrows to the bottom of an empty bottle.

When…
in *that Day.*

You were <u>Liberated in **Christ**</u> from all sickness and disease. Come to the **Lord** and fall on **your** knees.

Gail P. Miller

When…
in *that Day.*

You were <u>Liberated in **Christ**</u> from all **your** sin, so **you** don't have to really give in.

When…
in *that Day.*

"But beloved, do not forget this one thing that with the Lord one day is as a thousand years, and a thousand years as one day."

When the Day of Pentecost had fully come, <u>Liberation **in** Christ</u> was **fully** won.

This is That Day!

Acts 2:1
II Corinthians 3:17
II Peter 3:8

True Love Has a Passion for You!

What Do You Want?
(Words of Knowledge and Exhortation)

What **you** want is **Jesus.**

What **you** want is to see **God's** face in peace.

What **you** want is to partake of **His Love.**

What **you** want is to receive the **Spirit of Truth**

What **you** want is eternal **Life.**

What **you** want is a one-on-one encounter with the **Lord.**

God is the <u>only</u> **One** authorized to give **you** what **you** want.

So… what do **you** want?

Deuteronomy 30:15-20
John 14:6
John 16:13-15
John 17: 2-3

Gail P. Miller

Divine Revelation

The **Lord** revealed to me that one of the main reasons my **father** joined a secret society, organizations and other groups was to prove **his manhood** to those who had judged him as less than a man. He wanted to validate his self-worth by being a part of a group that would accept him for who he was, including the color of his skin. What my dad did not know at the time was, as a **black man**, his **manhood** was not defined by family, friends, society, the world or by the things that he possessed; but by **God** who gave him his **manliness** at creation. Once **God** finished with my dad and us in the beginning, **He** said, "It [my dad and all of us] was very good." (Genesis 1:31)

God judged my **father** by his obedience to **Him, His Word** and by how he taught, trained and lead by example the gifts **God** had given **him; his** children. **God,** I believe that this understanding will liberate men like my **father** in their hearts and minds. Those **black men** who were born during my **father's** era, the early 1900s, to this present age who have the same self-worth, value systems and quest to validate manhood.

I am truly blessed to say my **father**, George N. Miller Sr., who lived from February 1, 1917 to May 22, 2004, took great care in handling **God's** business concerning his children, grandchildren and great-grandchildren. Seek the **Lord, men of color,** to find out how to care for the gifts **He** has given **you** therefore, who you are and your worth can only be found in the heart of **God** who is your true guest.

> "And you, fathers, do not provoke your children to wrath, but bring them up in the training and admonition of the Lord."
> —Ephesians 6:4

I pray **God** will give **you** the deliverance needed to move **you** forward in **Him** and life. To know that salvation affords **you** the acceptance you have been thirsting for and that **you** have **His** eye, ear and presence made available to **you** if **you** seek to know **Him**…**His Way!**

Gail P. Miller

My Father

If **you** asked me, "What kind of **man** was my **father**?" I would say **he** was:

> A **man** who loved **his** God.
> A **man** who loved **his** wife.
> A **man** who loved **his** family.
> A **man** who loved **his** church.
> A **man** who loved **his** pastor.
> A **man** who loved **his** friends.
> A **man** who loved **his** neighbor.
> A **man** who loved **his** country.

> How was my **father**?

> A **man** who was humble.
> A **man** who was responsible.
> A **man** who was faithful.
> A **man** who was diligent.
> A **man** who was dependable.
> A **man** who was time sensitive.
> A **man** who was reliable.
> A **man** who was a community activist.
> A **man** who was practical.
> A **man** who was logical.
> A **man** who was capable.
> A **man** who was giving.
> A **man** who was caring.
> A **man** who was always there.
> A **man** who was a gentleman.

True Love Has a Passion for You!

A **man** who was funny.
A **man** who was quick-witted.
A **man** who lead by example.

How would I describe my **father**?

A **man** who worked.
A **man** who had some faults.
A **man** who could fix anything.
A **man** who counted the cost.
A **man** who spoke **his** mind.
A **man** who lived life to its fullest.
A **man** who made **you** laugh.
A **man** who told **you** when **you** were wrong.
A **man** who came to **you**r aide anytime of the day or night.

What were the characteristics of my **father**?

A **man** of **God**,
A **man** of faith,
A **man** of peace,
A **man** of values,
A **man** of morals,
A **man** of passion,
A **man** of holiness,
A **man** of strength,
A **man** of integrity,
A **man** of **his** word,
A **man** of principle,
A **man** of quietness,
A **man** of confidence,
A **man** of preparation,
A **man** of intelligence,

Gail P. Miller

A **man** of righteousness,

In essence…my **father** was a **father**.
My **father** was a **Man!**

True Love Has a Passion for You!

Gail P. Miller

Bibliography

Thorndike/Barnhardt. *High School Dictionary*. Glenview IL: Scott, Foresman & Company, 1969.

True Love Has a Passion for You!

About Gail P. Miller

As she searched to find herself, Gail P. Miller drew upon her spirituality and life experiences. Her ordained quest uncovered that God is Relationship. From this revelation, sprang her God-given identity as His Utility Handmaiden.

She retired with 37 years of service as a physical education teacher in the Dayton Public Schools System.

She holds a bachelor's degree in physical education from Central State University and an associate's degree in ministry from Liberated in Christ School of Ministry. Under the tutelage of Dr. Diane M. Parks-Love, she is pursuing a bachelor's degree in ministry. Ms. Miller has answered the call as a prophet of God (Daughter of Thunder) to the nations.

Ms. Miller has one son and two grandsons. She resides in Dayton, Ohio.

True Love Has a Passion for You!
The Journal

What would you do for True Love?

Birthed out of a thirst to pursue God, the *True Love Has a Passion for You! Journal* provides answers into the search for spiritual self-discovery. This book guides you to embody the heart of God and understand that True Love seeks to ignite the gift in you. How? Relationship.

After reading this journal, you will find hidden treasures to help you
- ✟ Let go of the things that stifle True Love.
- ✟ Find liberty in True Love.
- ✟ Humble yourself to release the glory of True Love.
- ✟ Develop healthy natural and spiritual relationships.
- ✟ Uncover that God is Relationship.
- ✟ Discover the how, what and why to the book, *True Love Has a Passion for You!*

ISBN-13: 978-0-9794489-0-4
Retail price: $9.95

Gail P. Miller

Queen V Publishing
The Doorway to YOUR Destiny!

Go thou and publish abroad the kingdom of God.
—Luke 9:60

We are a contract publisher committed to transforming manuscripts into polished works of art. Queen V Publishing, a company of standard and integrity, offers an alternative that allows the word in YOU to do what it was sent to do for OTHERS.

Visit our website for submission guidelines and the plan that fits your publishing goals.

QueenVPublishing.com

We help experts master self-publishing!

888.802.1802

True Love Has a Passion for You!

Pen of the Writer

*Out of Ephraim was there a root of them against Amalek; after thee, Benjamin, among thy people; out of Machir came down governors, and out of Zebulun they that handle the **pen of the writer**.*
—Judges 5:14

Pen Of the WritER

A publishing company committed to using the writing pen as a weapon to fight the enemy and celebrate the good news of Christ Jesus.

Self-Publishing Made Easy Journals
Mentoring
Publishing
Free Your Mind and the Words Will Follow Writers Retreat
Pen of the Writer (POWER) Book Fest

Serving professional speakers and experts to magnify and monetize their message by publishing quality books.

Pen of the Writer, LLC
Dayton, Ohio
888.802.1802
info@PenOfTheWriter.com
PenOfTheWriter.com

Gail P. Miller

To order additional copies of
True Love Has a Passion for You!
or to schedule a speaking engagement, contact:

Gail P. Miller
PO Box 3751
Dayton, Ohio 45401-3751
937.269.1386
Miller-Gail@sbcglobal.net

* *

Mail copies of *True Love Has a Passion for You!* to

Name:	
Address:	
Phone:	
Email:	

Quantity	Price Per Book	Total
	$12.95	
Sales Tax (Ohio residents add $0.97 per book)		
Shipping ($3.49 first book, $0.99 each add'l)		
Grand Total (money orders only*)		

* Make payable to Gail P. Miller

** Please allow four weeks to process your order **

Also available on Amazon.com

True Love Has a Passion for You!